GET OVER IT!

CORINNE MUCHA

Get Over It! © 2014 Corinne Mucha
Published by Secret Acres
Designed by Corinne Mucha

Secret Acres
237 Flatbush Ave, # 331
Brooklyn, NY 11217

Printed in USA

Special thanks to: Sam, Heather Radke,
Kate McGroarty, Sarah Holtschlag,
Sarah Becan, good ol' Mom + Dad,
Barry Matthews + Leon Avelino
and the Vermont Studio Center

Library of Congress PCN: 2013956598

ISBN-13: 978-0-9888149-6-7
ISBN-10: 0-9888149-6-X

SA027

· INTRODUCTION ·

When I was 23, I moved from Massachusetts to Chicago.

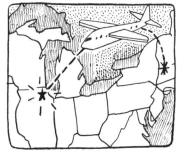

I followed my boyfriend, Sam, who was following a creative project.

I joked that I relocated because I heard the streets of the Windy City were paved with gold.

But really, I moved for love.

Still, I assumed our future was golden. A shiny, sure thing.

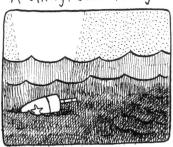

Smooth sailing forever.

We got a nice apartment. We played at being grownups.

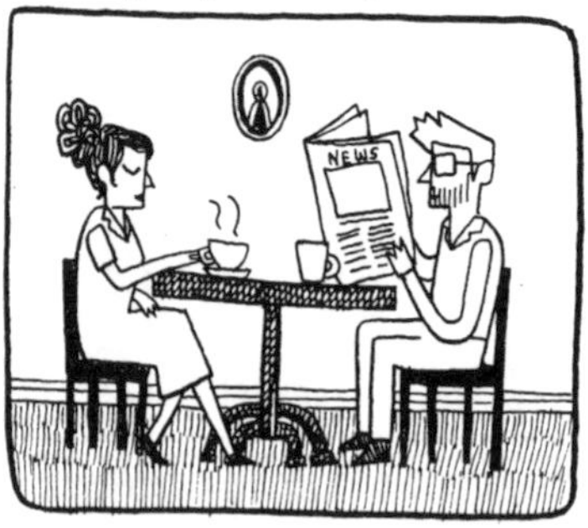
NEWS

We settled into our home the way children build a fort: pulling objects from every corner of the city, every alley.

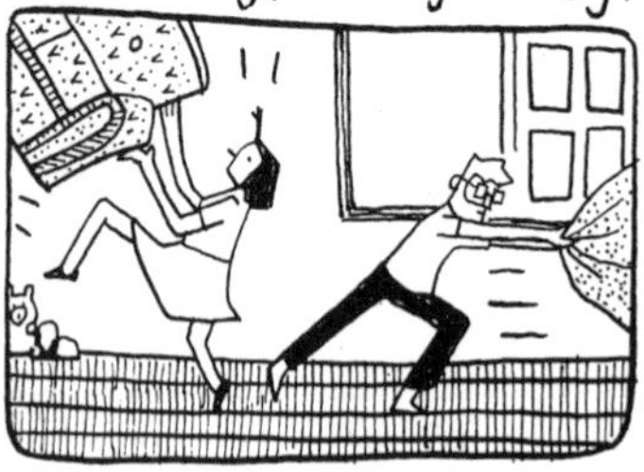

We were done with college. We studied new lessons in uncertainty.

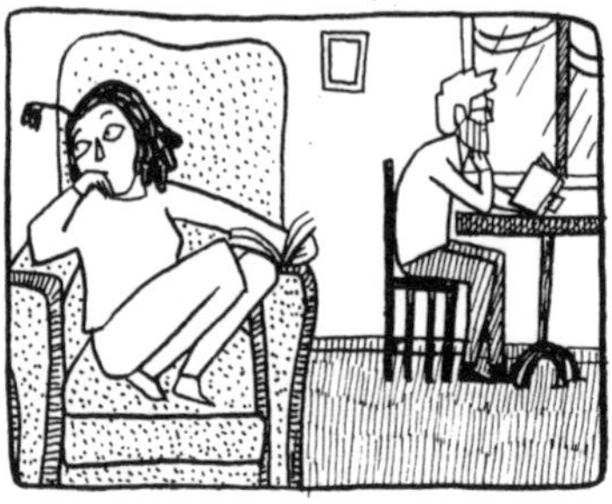

We got jobs we hated. We watched money do its disappearing trick.

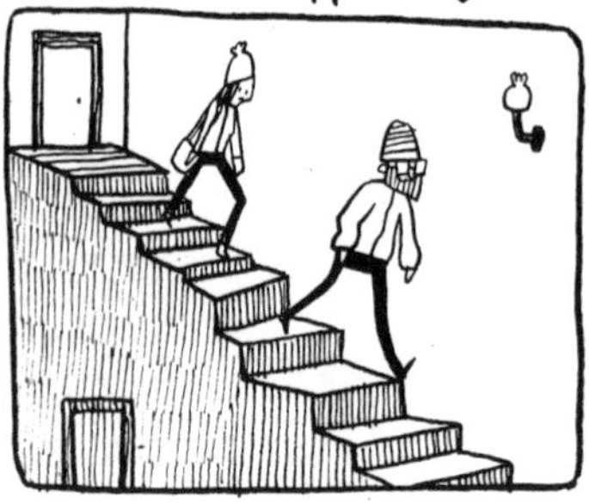

Five months after my arrival, nearly 3 years into our relationship, we broke up.

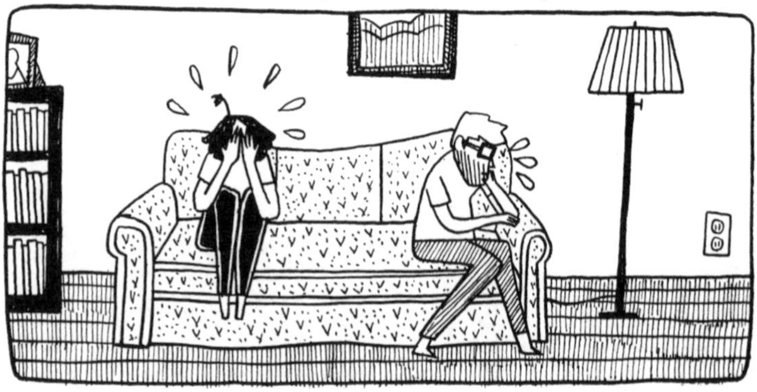

I hate the term "BREAK UP." It suggests something neat happened, something clear.

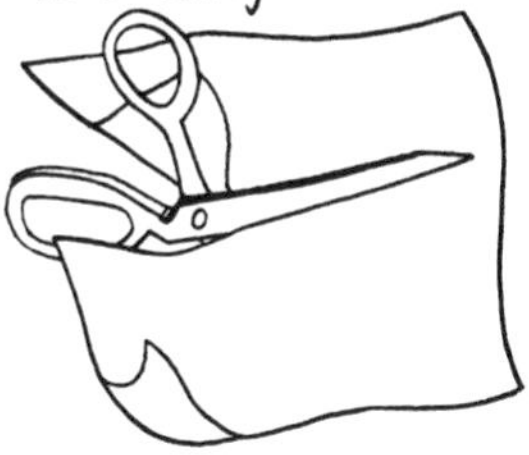

It conjures images of ruined china, a delicate plate split in two.

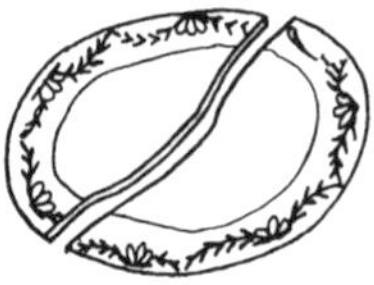

But breakups are rarely clean like porcelain. There are no sweepable shards.

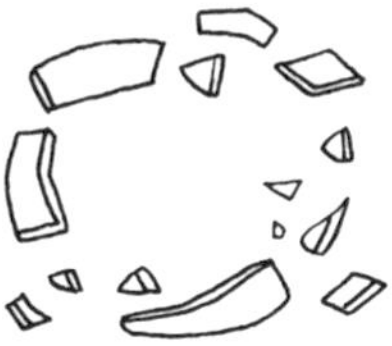

Breakups are the division of a dinner set, a functioning whole, separated.

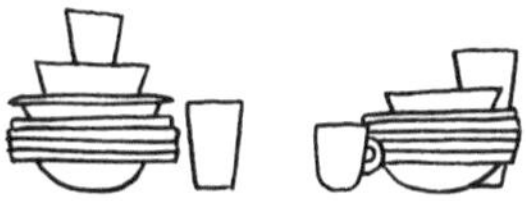

A rip in the tablecloth, an unraveling seam.

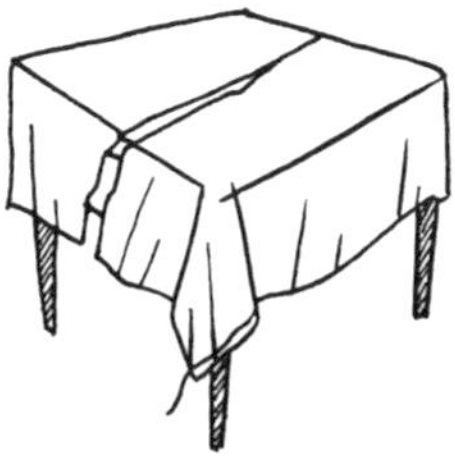

THIS is a breakup story, the saga of one relationship's undoing.

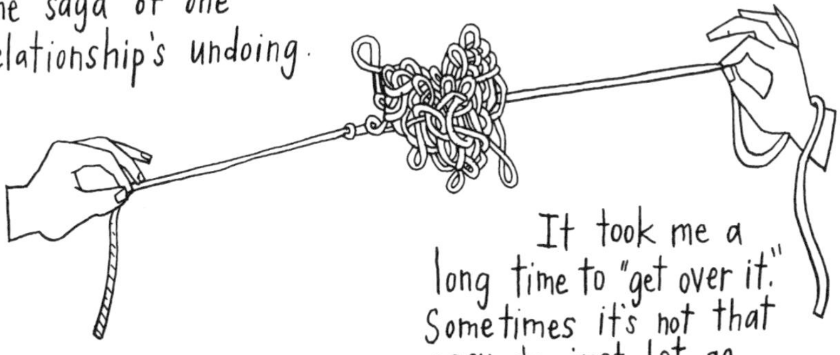

It took me a long time to "get over it." Sometimes it's not that easy to just let go.

Part One

EVERYTHING IN ITS PLACE
ASTERIOS POLYP
GRAPHIC FICTION
GIRL STORIES
SEW
Hey Penguin spotter — these found rocks cool rocks I thought you'd like. ♥ Sam
CRAYOLA
Buttface, Here, I drew you this heart-shaped poop. xoxo, C
10 THINGS I LOVE ABOUT YOU
S - FOR YOU
COOL BATMA
PUG wearing LIPSTICK
Go to bed?
Ok.

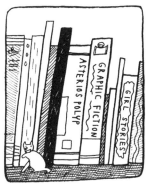

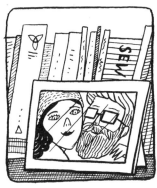

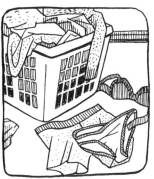

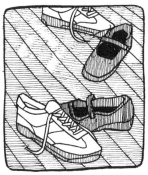

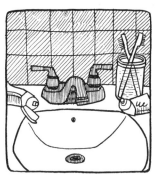

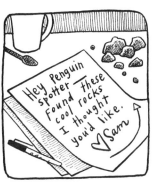

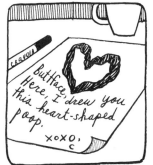

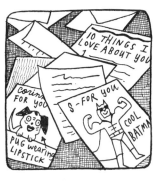

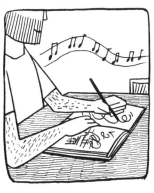

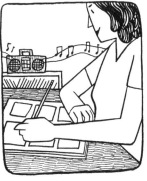

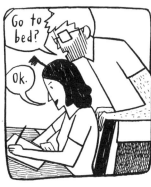

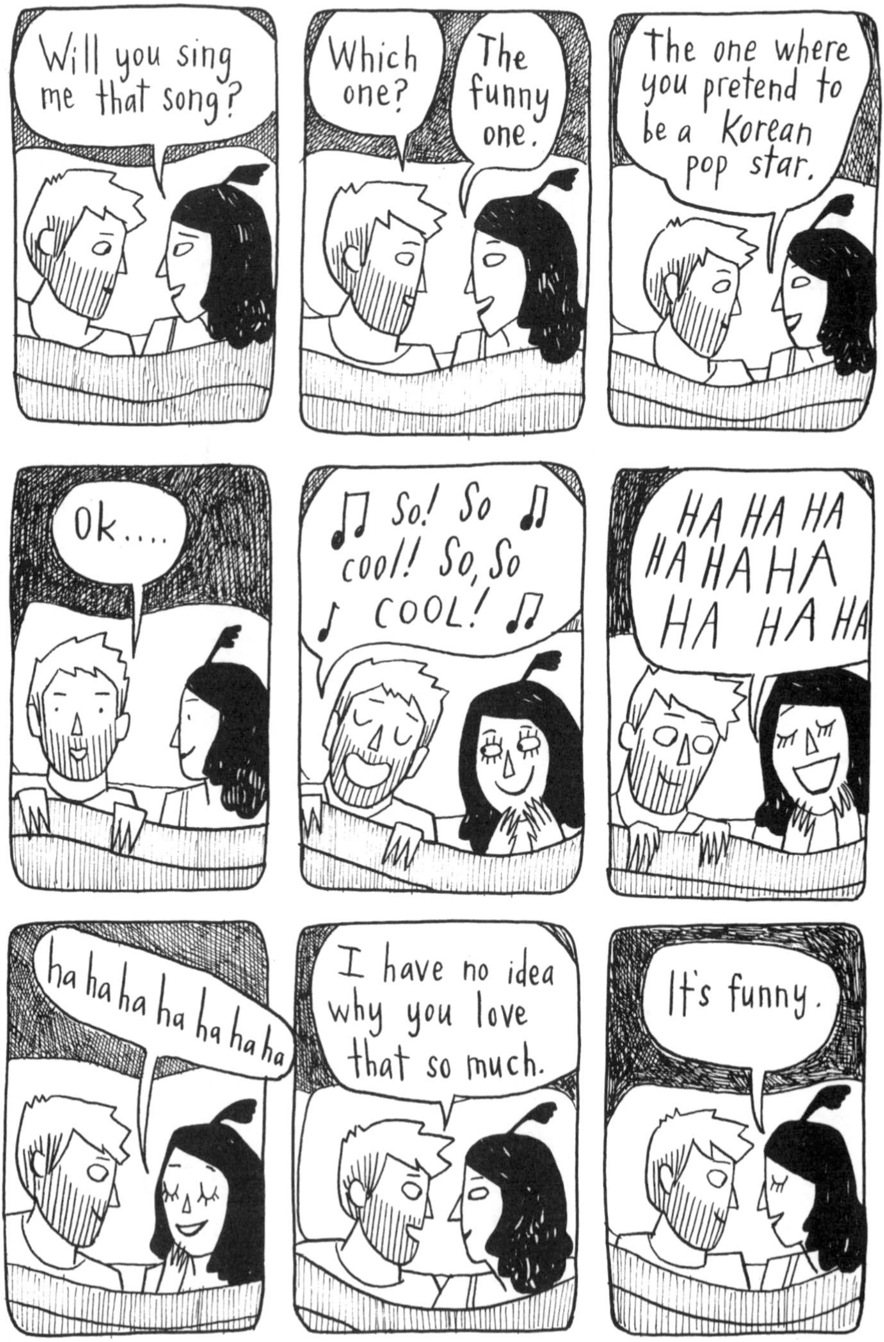
Will you sing me that song?
Which one?
The funny one.
The one where you pretend to be a Korean pop star.
Ok....
♫ So! So ♫ cool! So, So ♩ COOL! ♫
HA HA HA HA HA HA HA HA HA
ha ha ha ha ha ha ha ha
I have no idea why you love that so much.
It's funny.

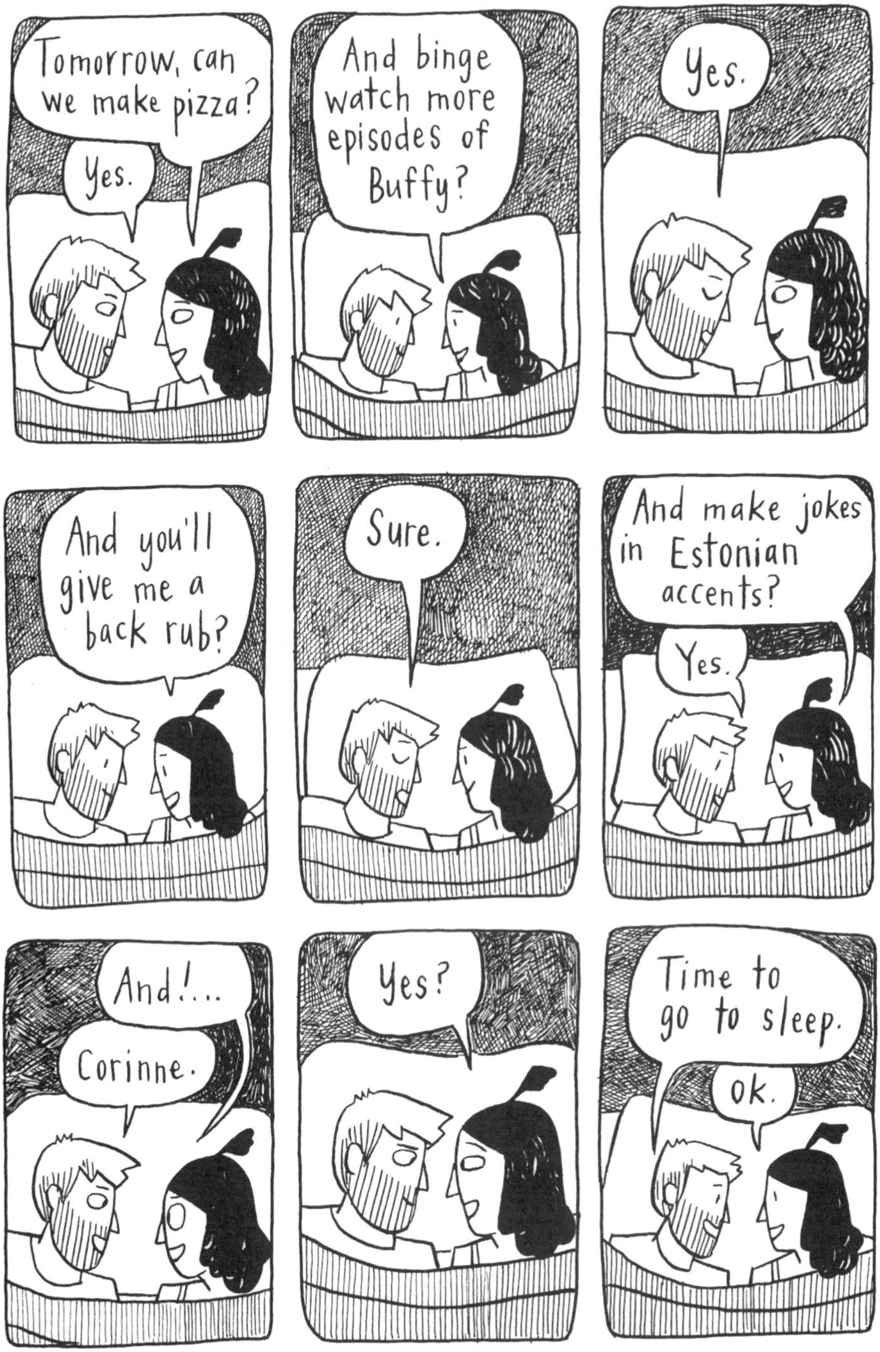
Tomorrow, can we make pizza?
Yes.
And binge watch more episodes of Buffy?
Yes.
And you'll give me a back rub?
Sure.
And make jokes in Estonian accents?
Yes.
And!...
Corinne.
Yes?
Time to go to sleep.
Ok.

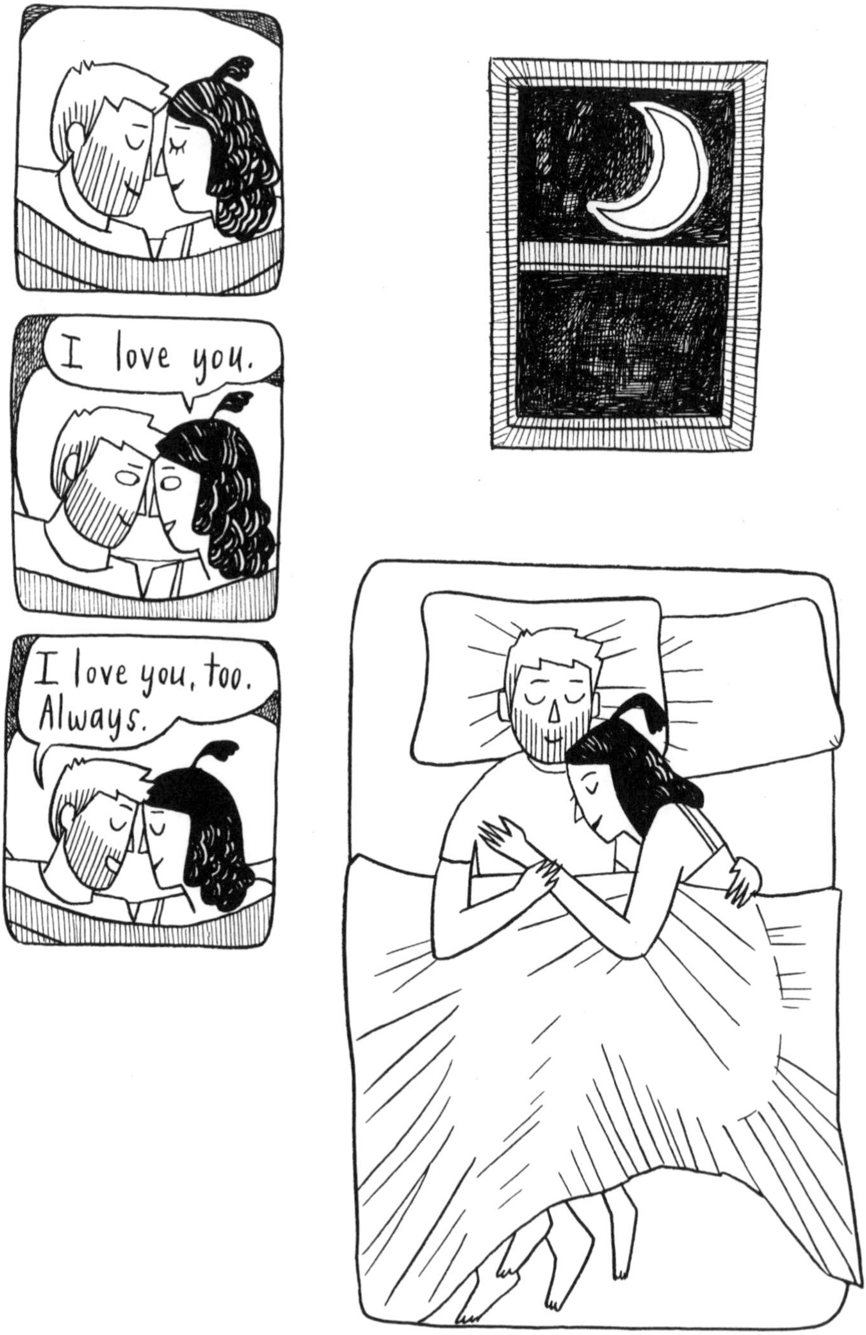
I love you.
I love you, too. Always.

THE BEGINNING of the END

Sometimes it starts with a question...

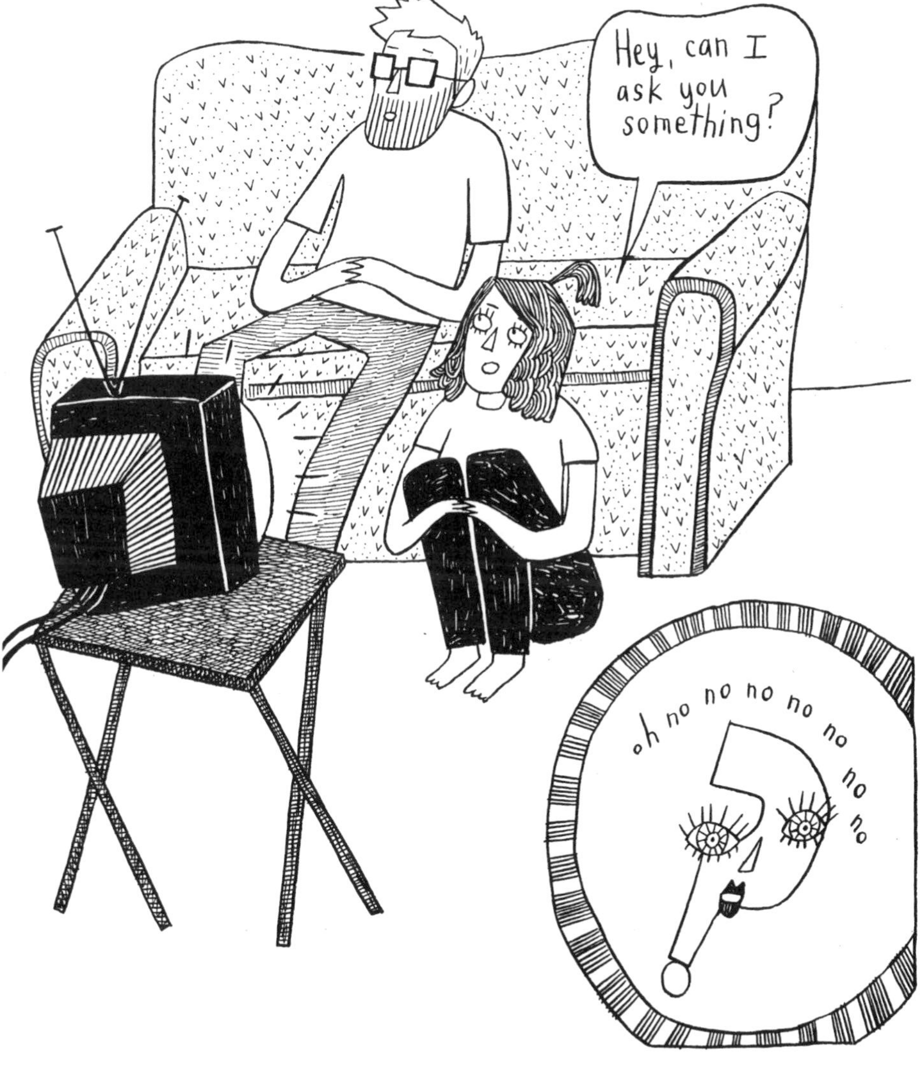
Hey, can I ask you something?
oh no no no no no no no no

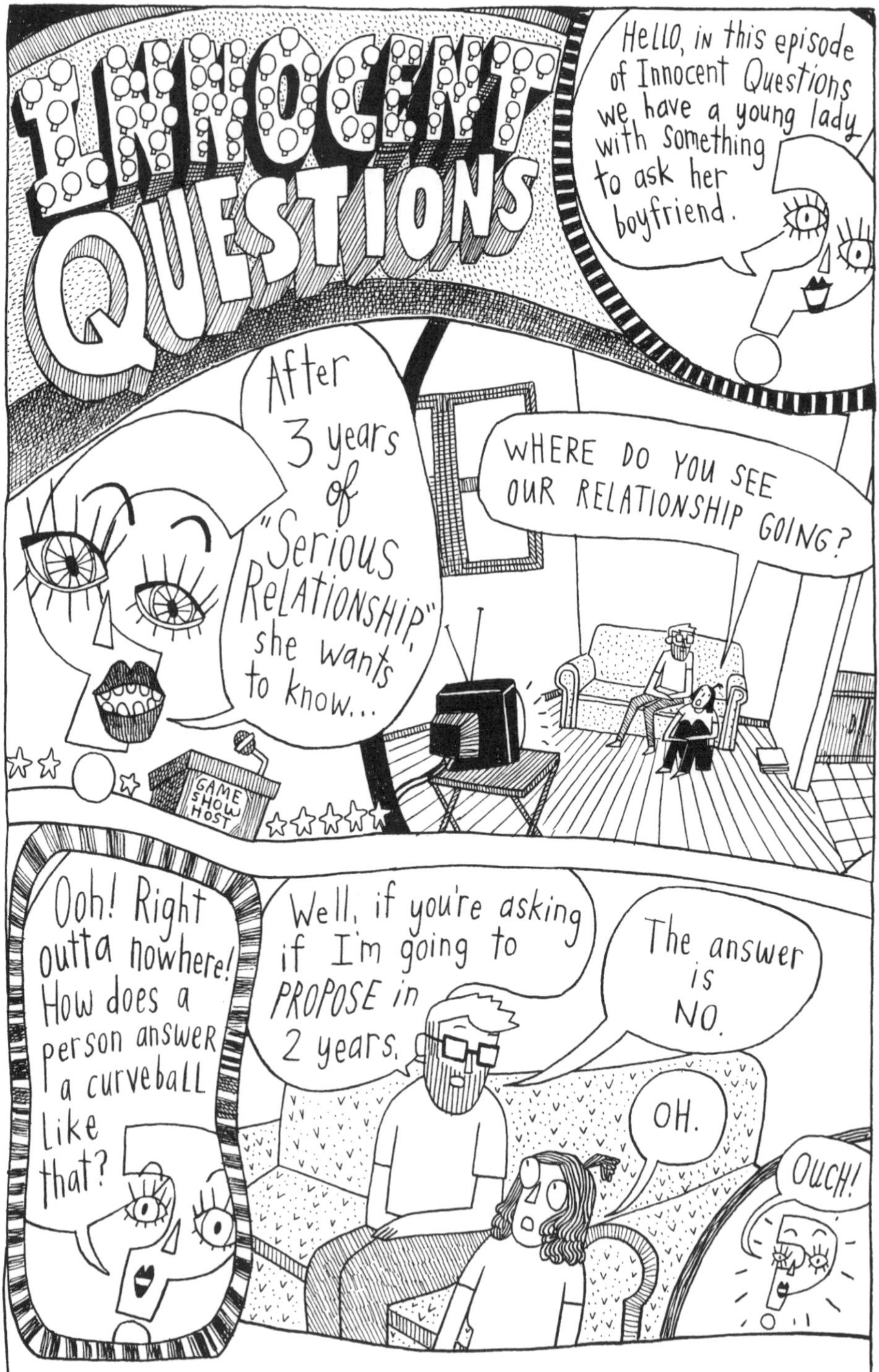
INNOCENT QUESTIONS
HELLO, IN this episode of Innocent Questions we have a young lady with something to ask her boyfriend.
After 3 years of "Serious RELATIONSHIP," she wants to know...
GAME SHOW HOST
WHERE DO YOU SEE OUR RELATIONSHIP GOING?
Ooh! Right outta nowhere! How does a person answer a curveball like that?
Well, if you're asking if I'm going to PROPOSE in 2 years.
The answer is NO.
OH.
OUCH!

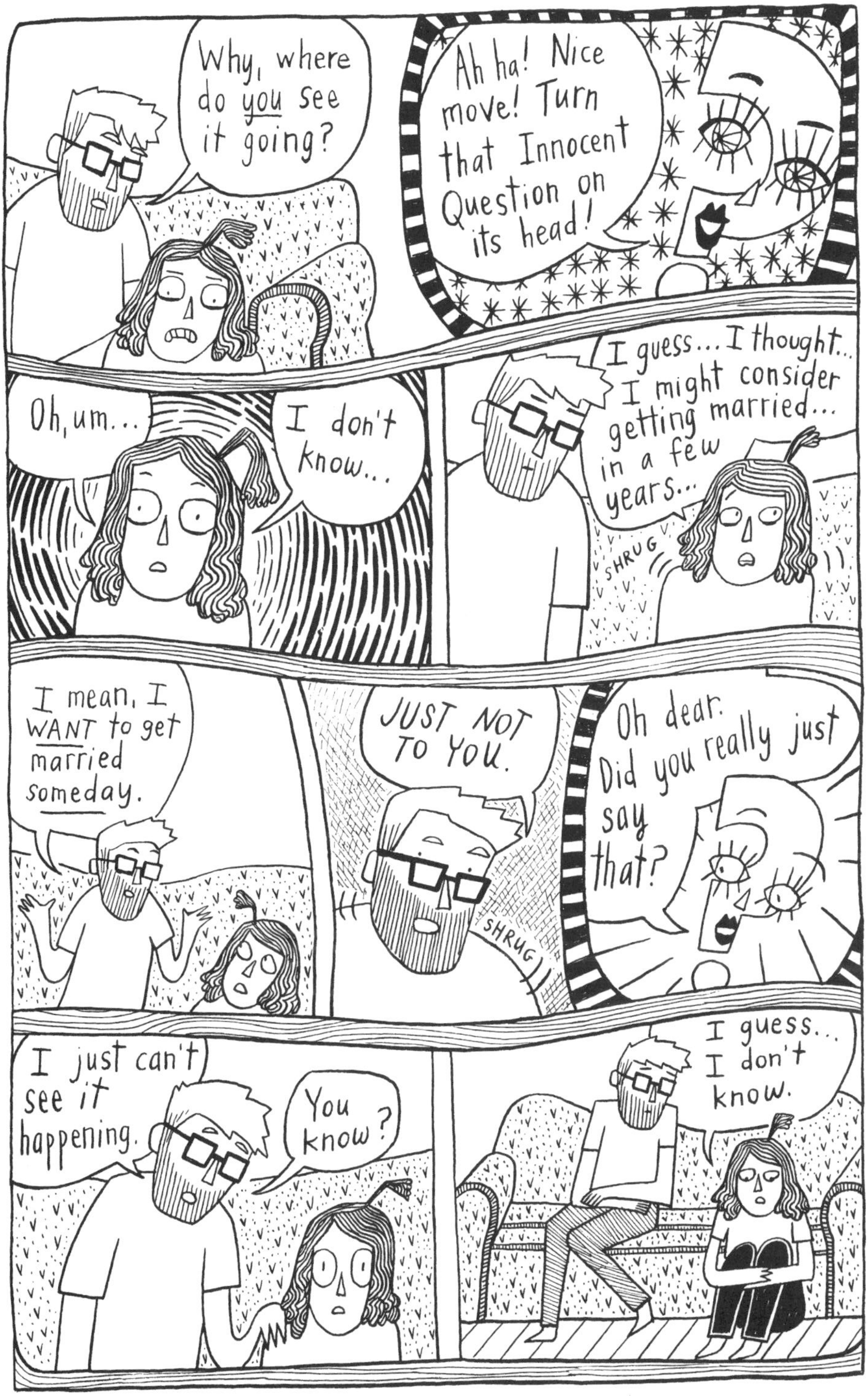

Why, where do you see it going?
Ah ha! Nice move! Turn that Innocent Question on its head!
Oh, um...
I don't know...
I guess... I thought... I might consider getting married... in a few years...
SHRUG
I mean, I WANT to get married someday.
JUST NOT TO YOU.
SHRUG
Oh dear. Did you really just say that?
I just can't see it happening.
You know?
I guess... I don't know.

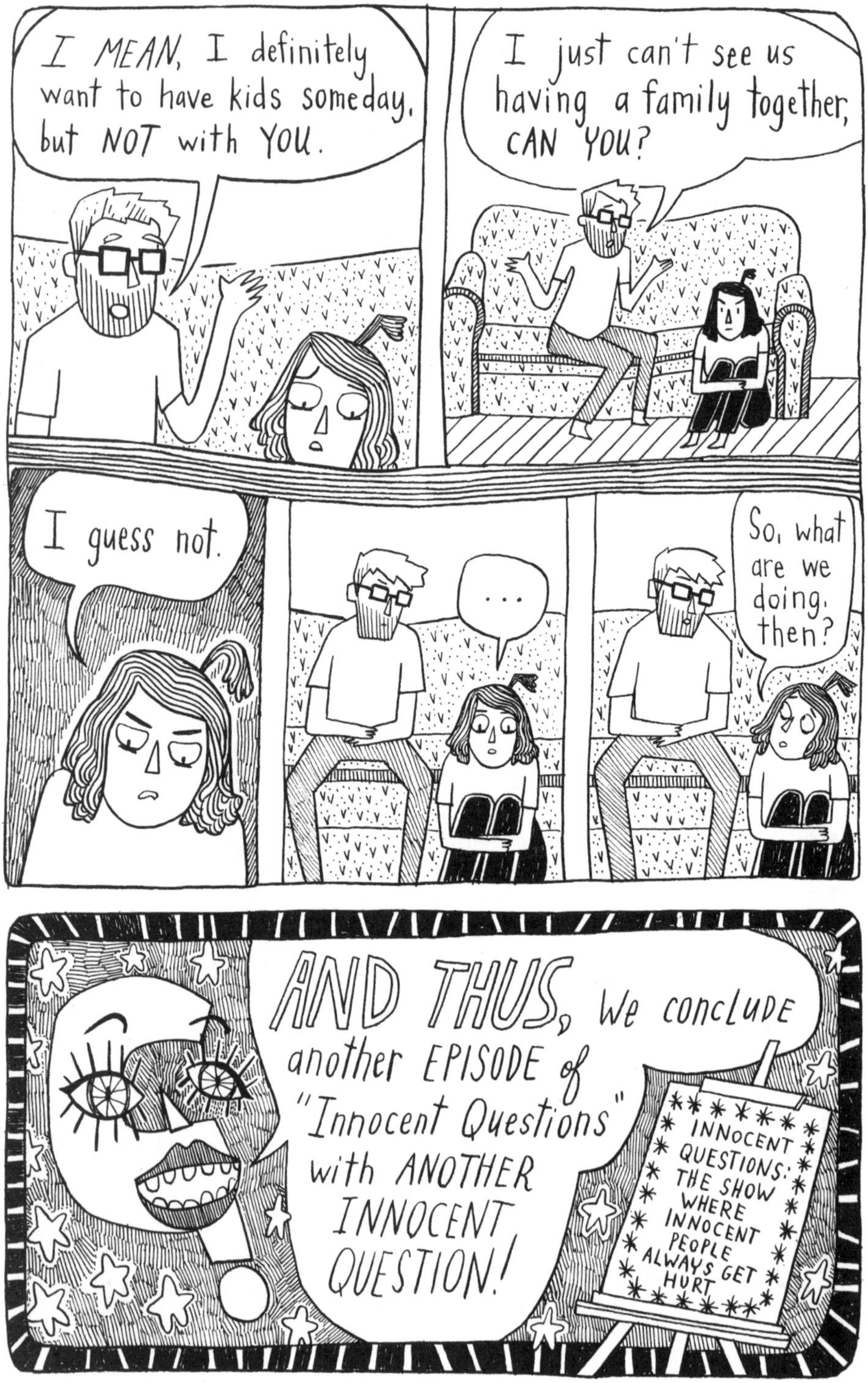
I MEAN, I definitely want to have kids someday, but NOT with YOU.
I just can't see us having a family together, CAN YOU?
I guess not.
. . .
So, what are we doing, then?
AND THUS, we conclude another EPISODE of "Innocent Questions" with ANOTHER INNOCENT QUESTION!
INNOCENT QUESTIONS: THE SHOW WHERE INNOCENT PEOPLE ALWAYS GET HURT

(commercial break)

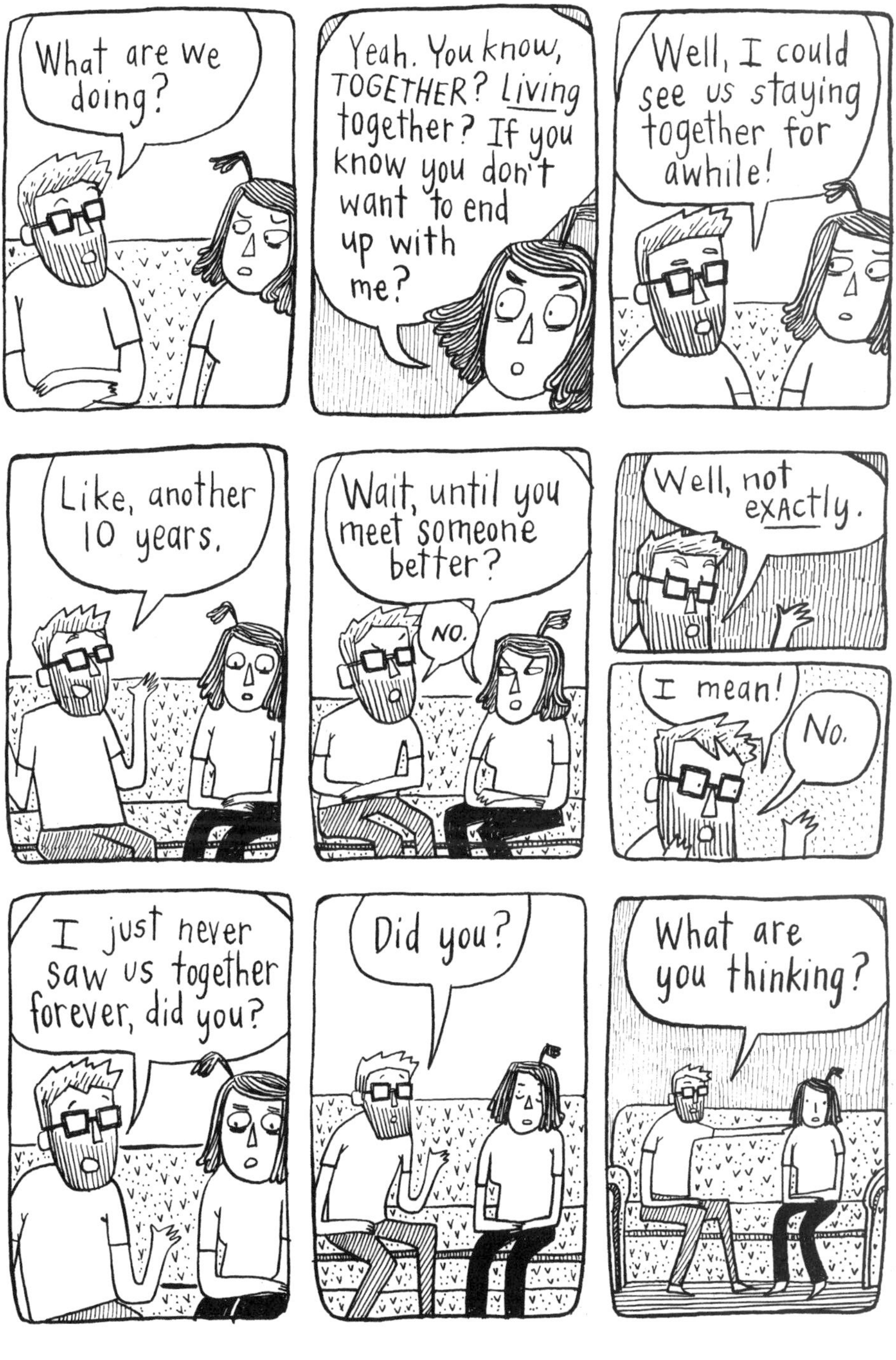
What are we doing?
Yeah. You know, TOGETHER? Living together? If you know you don't want to end up with me?
Well, I could see us staying together for awhile!
Like, another 10 years.
Wait, until you meet someone better?
NO.
Well, not exactly.
I mean!
No.
I just never saw us together forever, did you?
Did you?
What are you thinking?

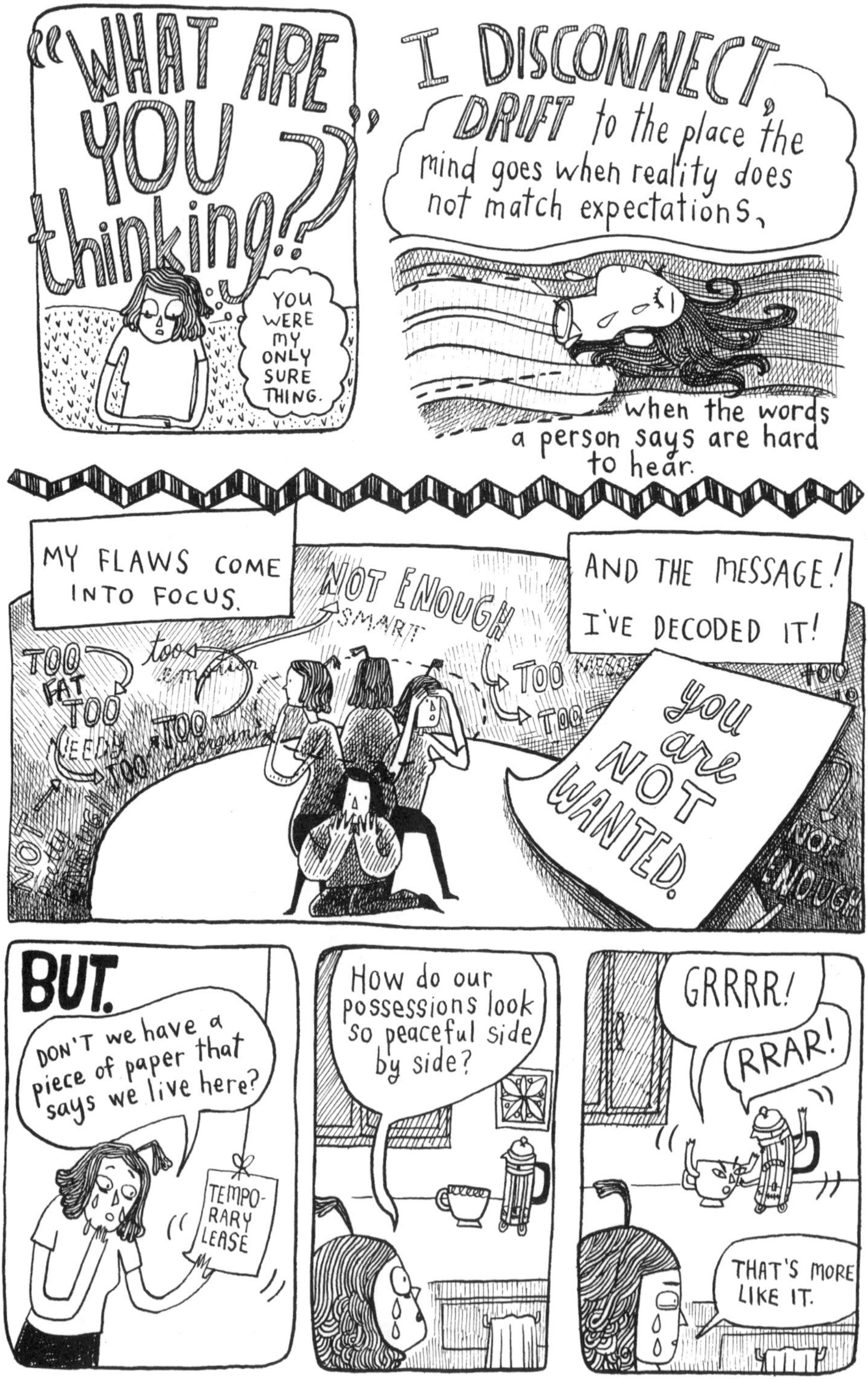
"WHAT ARE YOU thinking??"
YOU WERE MY ONLY SURE THING.
I DISCONNECT,
DRIFT to the place the mind goes when reality does not match expectations,
when the words a person says are hard to hear.
MY FLAWS COME INTO FOCUS.
AND THE MESSAGE! I'VE DECODED IT!
NOT ENOUGH
SMART
TOO FAT
TOO NEEDY
TOO
TOO
TOO
TOO
YOU ARE NOT WANTED.
NOT ENOUGH
BUT.
DON'T we have a piece of paper that says we live here?
TEMPORARY LEASE
How do our possessions look so peaceful side by side?
GRRRR!
RRAR!
THAT'S MORE LIKE IT.

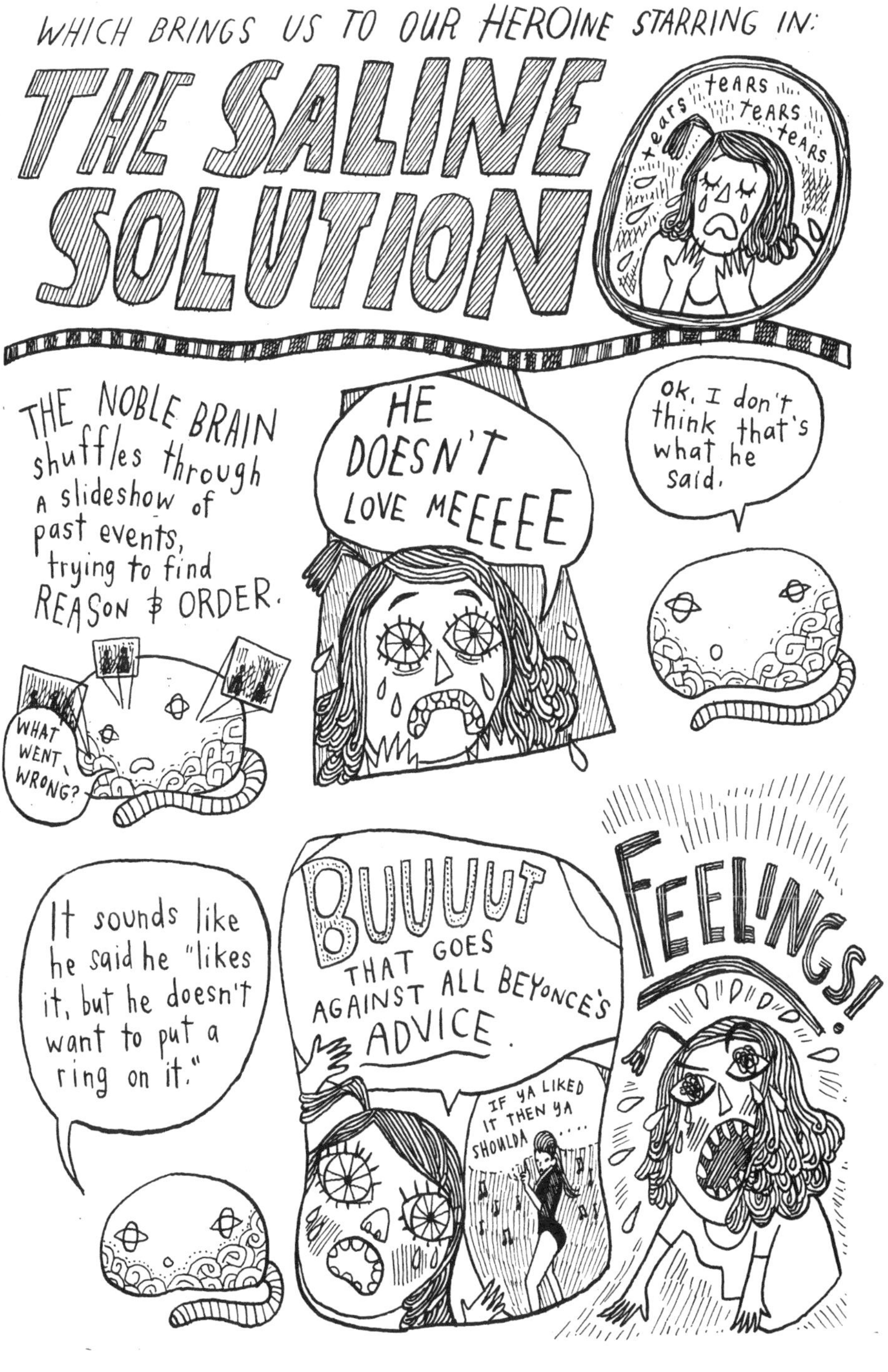
WHICH BRINGS US TO OUR HEROINE STARRING IN:
THE SALINE SOLUTION
tears tears tears tears
THE NOBLE BRAIN shuffles through a slideshow of past events, trying to find REASON & ORDER.
WHAT WENT WRONG?
HE DOESN'T LOVE MEEEEE
Ok, I don't think that's what he said.
It sounds like he said he "likes it, but he doesn't want to put a ring on it."
BUUUUT THAT GOES AGAINST ALL BEYONCE'S ADVICE.
IF YA LIKED IT THEN YA SHOULDA....
FEELINGS!

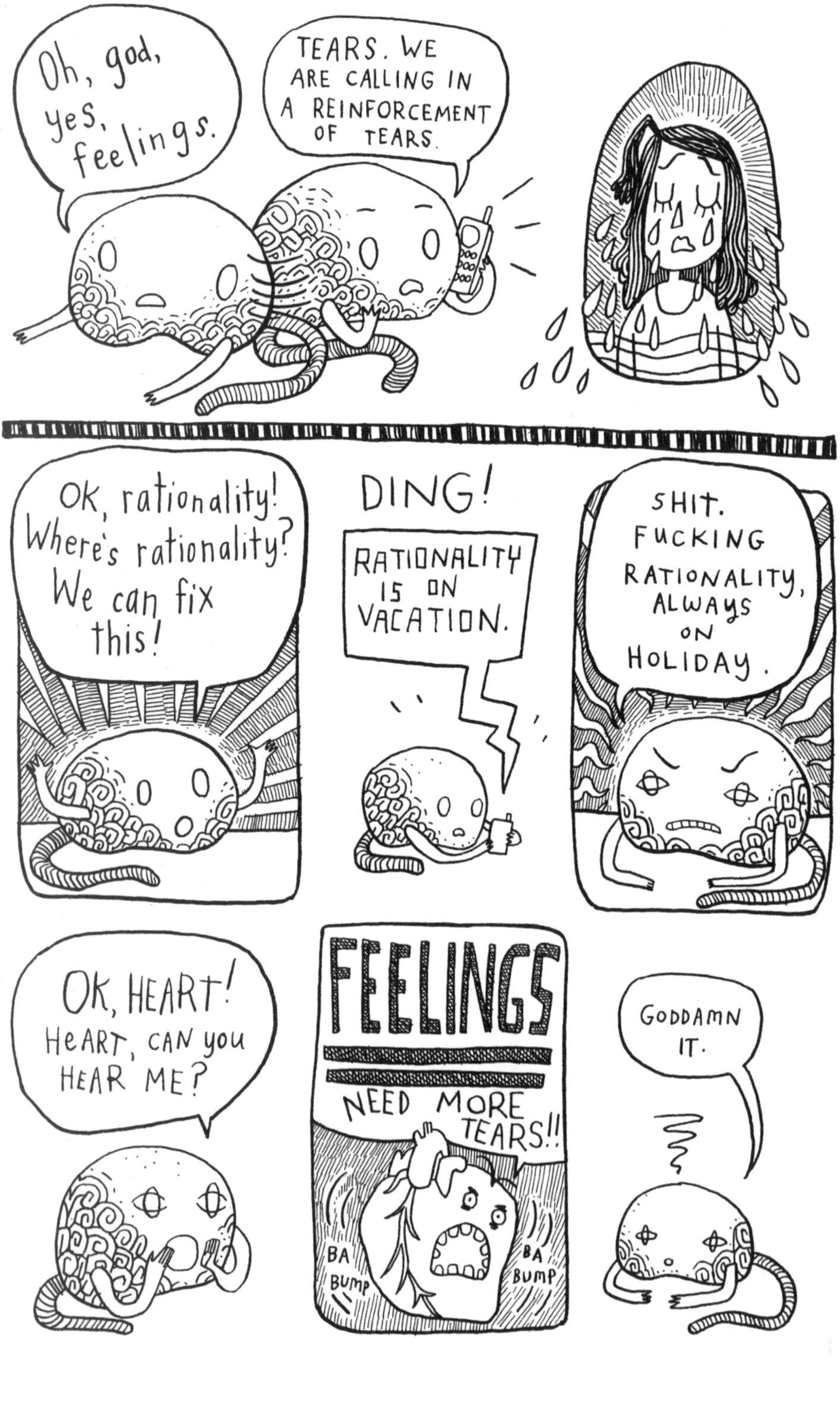
Oh, god, yes, feelings.
TEARS. WE ARE CALLING IN A REINFORCEMENT OF TEARS.
OK, rationality! Where's rationality? We can fix this!
DING!
RATIONALITY IS ON VACATION.
SHIT. FUCKING RATIONALITY, ALWAYS ON HOLIDAY.
OK, HEART! HEART, CAN YOU HEAR ME?
FEELINGS
NEED MORE TEARS!!
BA BUMP
BA BUMP
GODDAMN IT.

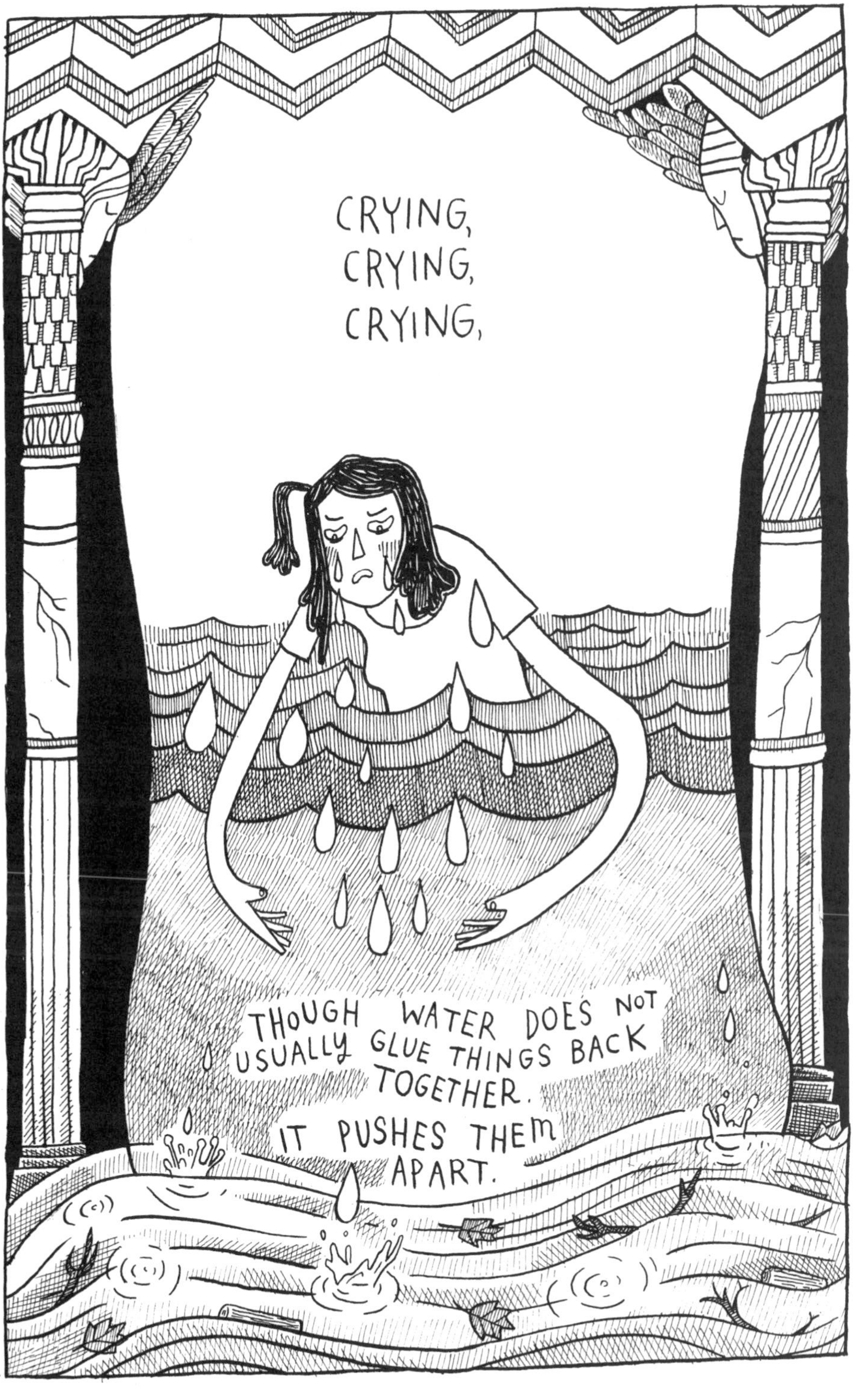
CRYING,
CRYING,
CRYING,
THOUGH WATER DOES NOT USUALLY GLUE THINGS BACK TOGETHER.
IT PUSHES THEM APART.

sniff
sniff

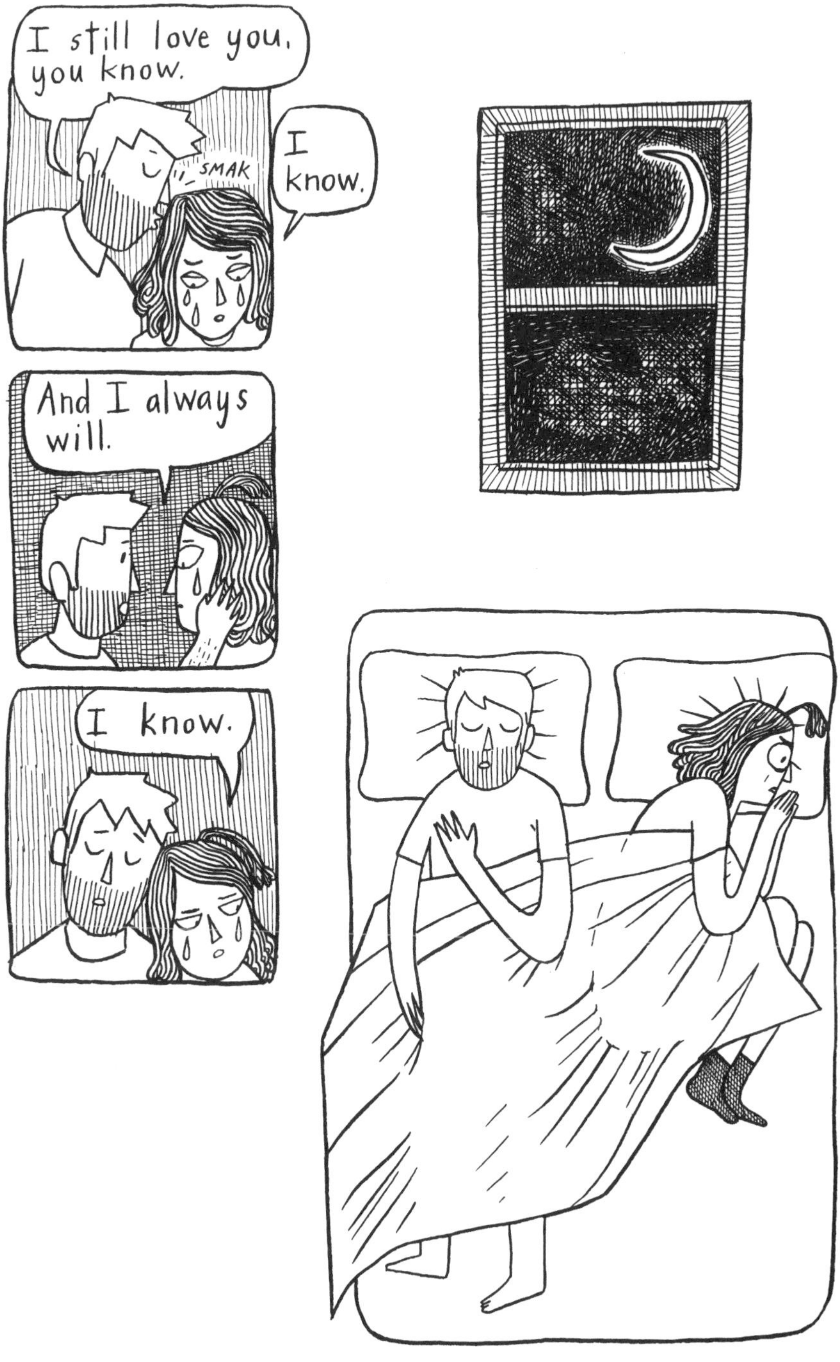
I still love you, you know.
SMAK
I know.
And I always will.
I know.

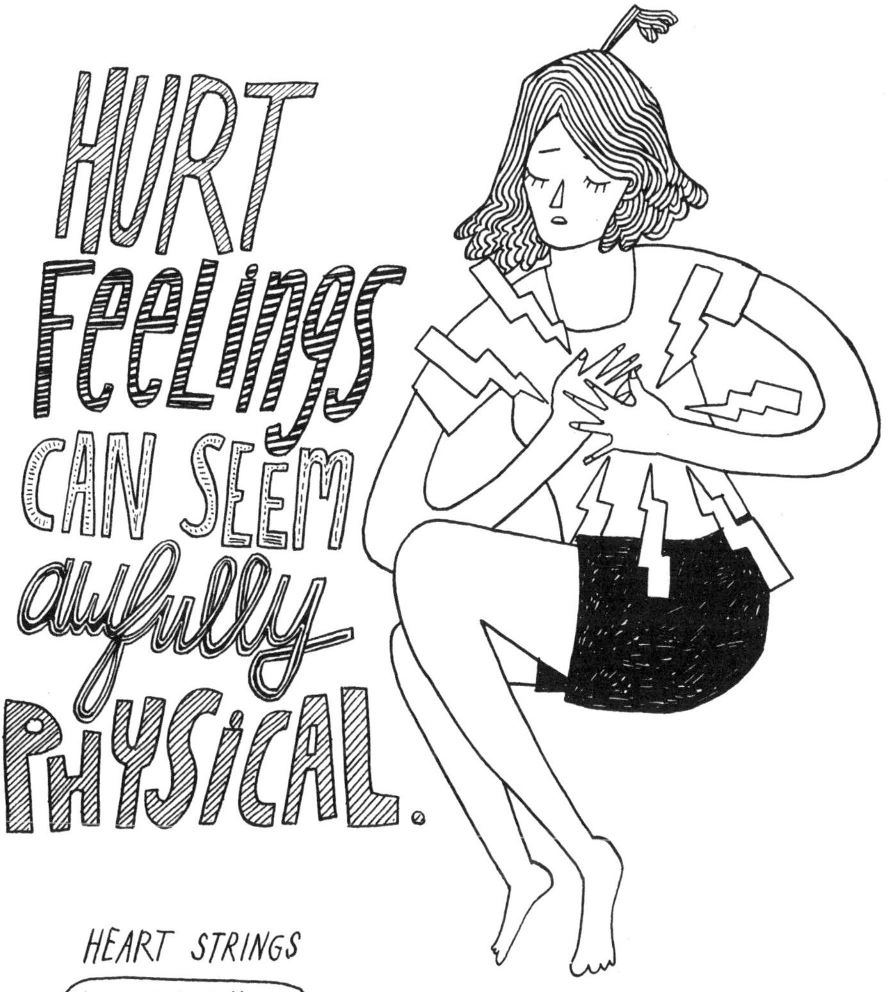
HURT
FEELINGS
CAN SEEM
awfully
PHYSICAL.

HEART STRINGS

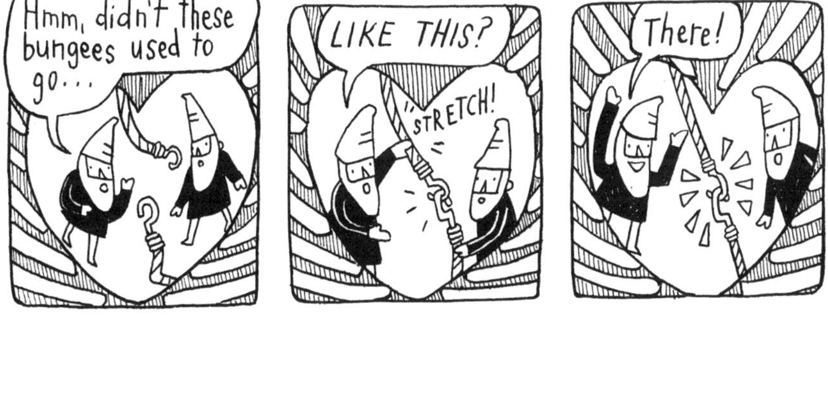
Hmm, didn't these bungees used to go...
LIKE THIS?
"STRETCH!"
There!

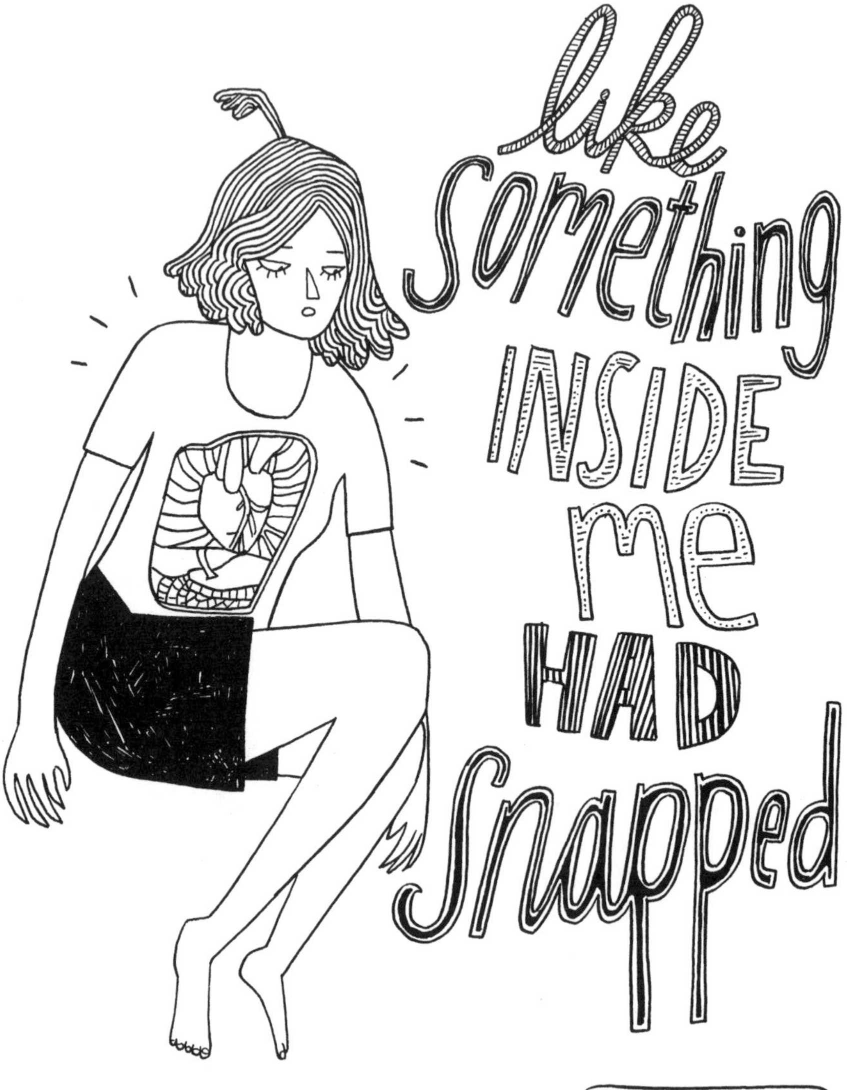
like
Something
INSIDE
me
HAD
Snapped

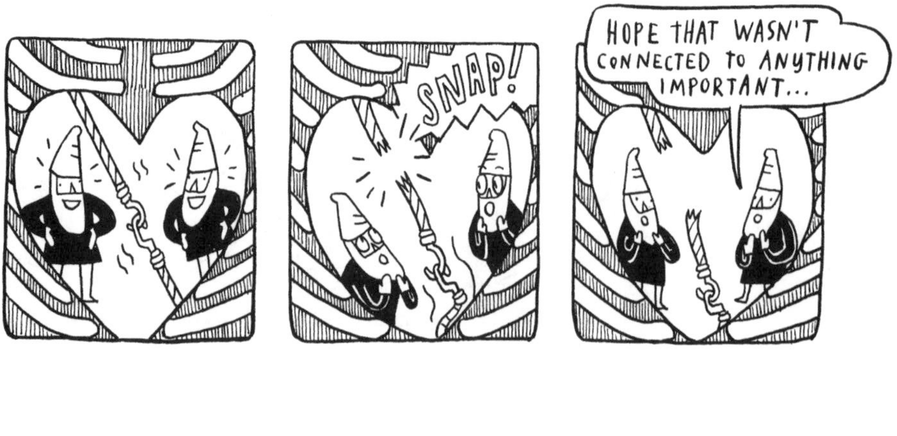
SNAP!
HOPE THAT WASN'T CONNECTED TO ANYTHING IMPORTANT...

AND THEN... SOMETHING DID POP.

OW.
That feels weird.
Guess I'll just ignore it.
trying to ignore just about every-thing right now.
NEXT DAY:
Huh. It really hurts to walk.

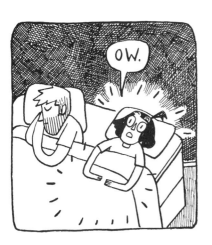

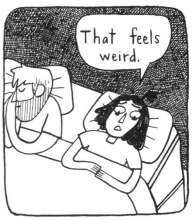

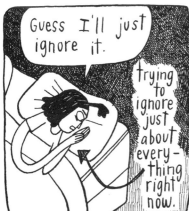

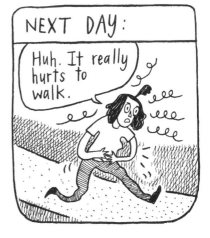

STEPS to ACHIEVING MEDICAL DIAGNOSIS:

#1 PHONE 5-6 GIRLFRIENDS

DO YOU THINK I JUST HAVE CRAMPS?

ARE YOU ON YOUR PERIOD?

NO.

THEN, NO.

#2 TRY A VARIETY OF NATURAL "REMEDIES"

WATER

KOMBUCHA

GINGER TEA

CHOCOLATE

#3 WATCH CHEESY MOVIE*

HOLLYWOOD, TAKE AWAY MY PAIN!

* THE PURSUIT OF HAPPYNESS

BY THE END OF THE MOVIE, SOMEONE WILL FALL IN LOVE, AND I WILL FEEL FINE!

end of movie...

OH GOD. WALKING. TOO PAINFUL.

#4 PHONE <u>ONE</u> MORE FRIEND. FINAL CONSULT.

DO YOU THINK I SHOULD GO TO THE HOSPITAL?

YEP. I'LL PICK YOU UP.

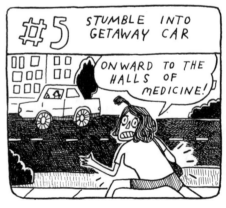

#5 STUMBLE INTO GETAWAY CAR

ONWARD TO THE HALLS OF MEDICINE!

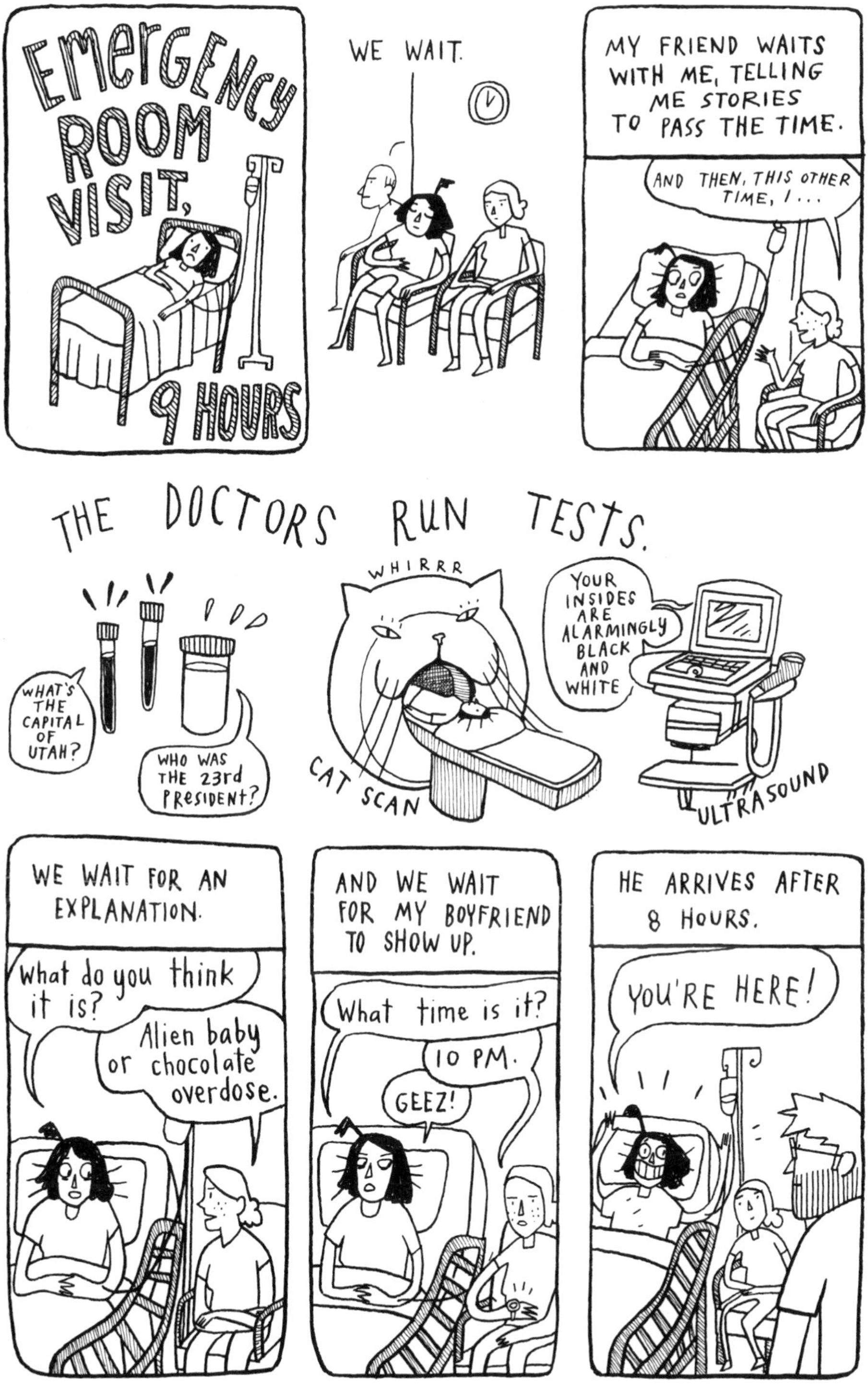
EMERGENCY ROOM VISIT, 9 HOURS
WE WAIT.
MY FRIEND WAITS WITH ME, TELLING ME STORIES TO PASS THE TIME.
AND THEN, THIS OTHER TIME, I...
THE DOCTORS RUN TESTS.
WHAT'S THE CAPITAL OF UTAH?
WHO WAS THE 23rd PRESIDENT?
WHIRRR
CAT SCAN
YOUR INSIDES ARE ALARMINGLY BLACK AND WHITE
ULTRASOUND
WE WAIT FOR AN EXPLANATION.
What do you think it is?
Alien baby or chocolate overdose.
AND WE WAIT FOR MY BOYFRIEND TO SHOW UP.
What time is it?
10 PM.
GEEZ!
HE ARRIVES AFTER 8 HOURS.
YOU'RE HERE!

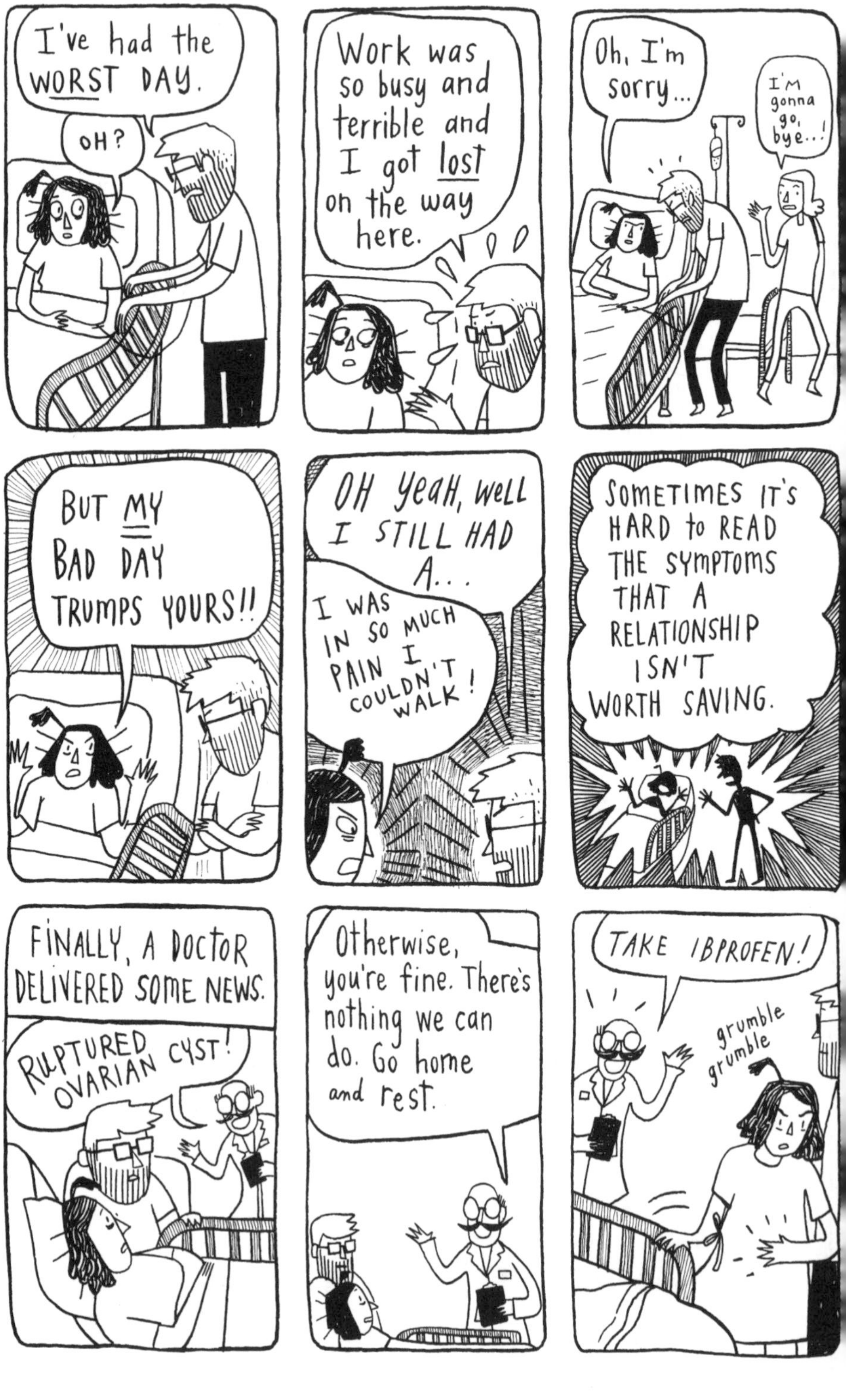
I've had the WORST DAY.
OH?
Work was so busy and terrible and I got lost on the way here.
Oh, I'm sorry...
I'M gonna go, bye...!
BUT MY BAD DAY TRUMPS YOURS!!
OH yeaH, WeLL I STILL HAD A...
I WAS IN SO MUCH PAIN I COULDN'T WALK!
SOMETIMES IT'S HARD to READ THE SYMPTOMS THAT A RELATIONSHIP ISN'T WORTH SAVING.
FINALLY, A DOCTOR DELIVERED SOME NEWS.
RUPTURED OVARIAN CYST!
Otherwise, you're fine. There's nothing we can do. Go home and rest.
TAKE IBPROFEN!
grumble grumble

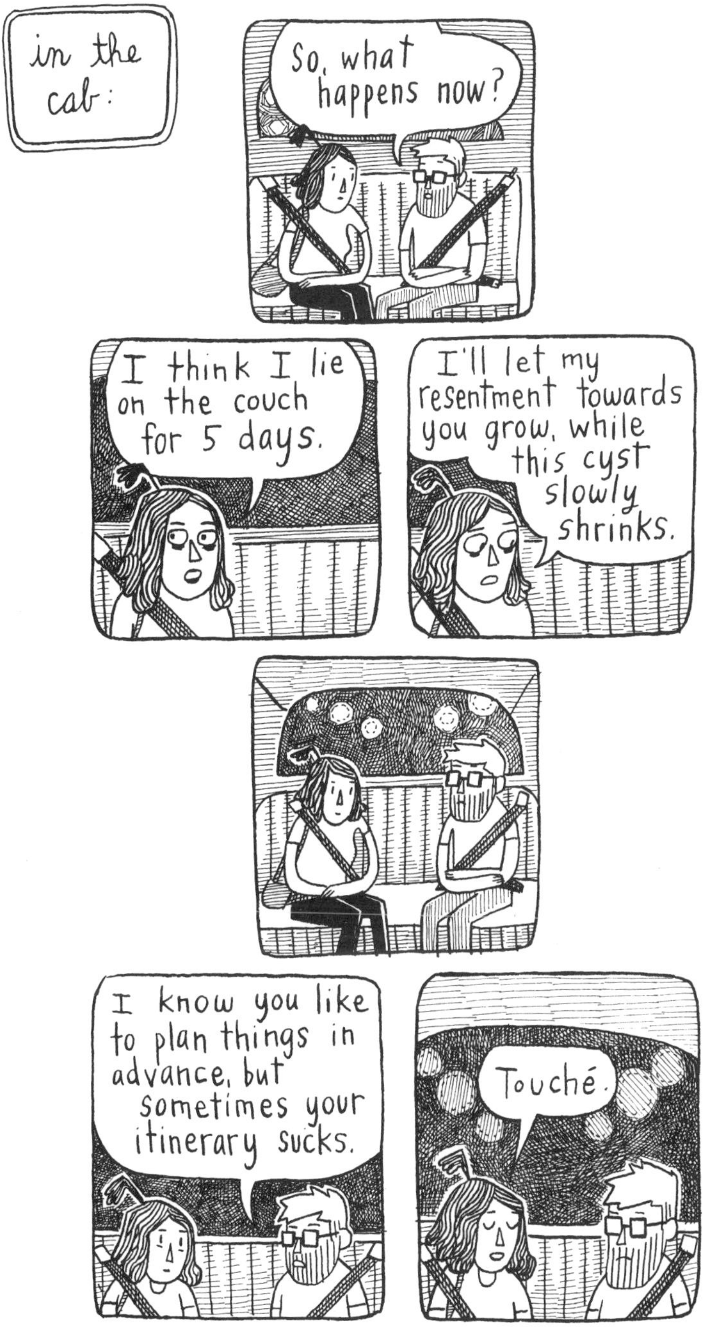
in the cab:
So, what happens now?
I think I lie on the couch for 5 days.
I'll let my resentment towards you grow, while this cyst slowly shrinks.
I know you like to plan things in advance, but sometimes your itinerary sucks.
Touché.

AN INTERLUDE from THE FUTURE

-OR- "MY BODY IS GOOD AT METAPHORS"

MONTHS LATER, MY ACCUPUNCTURIST EXPLAINED TO ME THE CONNECTION BETWEEN A BROKEN HEART AND A RUPTURED CYST.

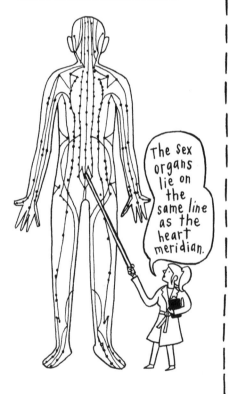

The sex organs lie on the same line as the heart meridian.

SO...POP!

AND POW!

It makes total sense that this happened to you.

OH.

Now let's stick some needles in you!

OK.

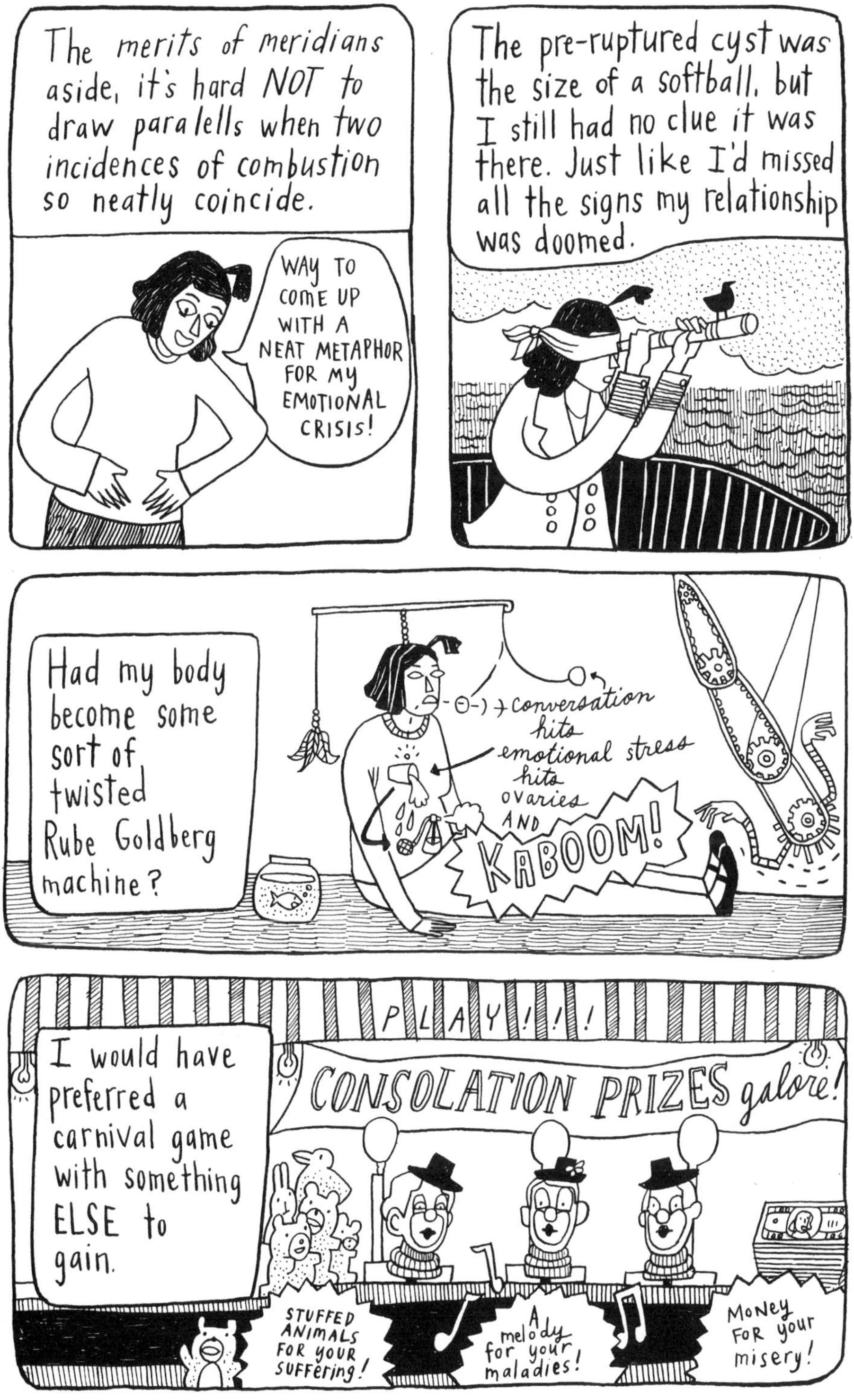
The merits of meridians aside, it's hard NOT to draw paralells when two incidences of combustion so neatly coincide.
WAY TO COME UP WITH A NEAT METAPHOR FOR MY EMOTIONAL CRISIS!
The pre-ruptured cyst was the size of a softball, but I still had no clue it was there. Just like I'd missed all the signs my relationship was doomed.
Had my body become some sort of twisted Rube Goldberg machine?
conversation
hits
emotional stress
hits
ovaries
AND
KABOOM!
PLAY!!!
I would have preferred a carnival game with something ELSE to gain.
CONSOLATION PRIZES galore!
STUFFED ANIMALS FOR YOUR SUFFERING!
A melody for your maladies!
MONEY FOR YOUR misery!

IN THE meantime,

I SIT STILL. MY BRAIN RUNS LAPS.

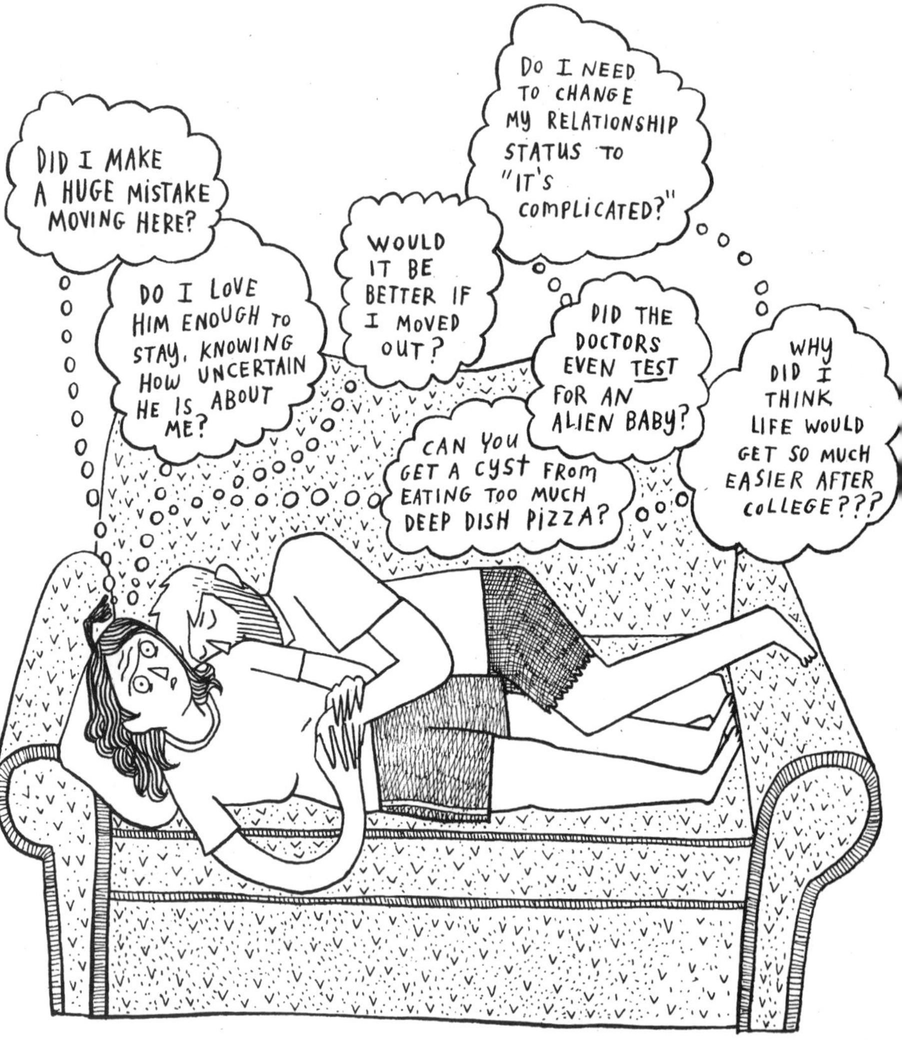

DID I MAKE A HUGE MISTAKE MOVING HERE?
DO I LOVE HIM ENOUGH TO STAY, KNOWING HOW UNCERTAIN HE IS ABOUT ME?
WOULD IT BE BETTER IF I MOVED OUT?
DO I NEED TO CHANGE MY RELATIONSHIP STATUS TO "IT'S COMPLICATED?"
DID THE DOCTORS EVEN TEST FOR AN ALIEN BABY?
CAN YOU GET A CYST FROM EATING TOO MUCH DEEP DISH PIZZA?
WHY DID I THINK LIFE WOULD GET SO MUCH EASIER AFTER COLLEGE???

SEVERAL WEEKS LATER:
"AND NOW WE SPLIT"
BREAKUP REDUX
I'm gonna move out!
But we can work things out!
I'M MAD!
I'M BREAKING UP WITH YOU!
I'm crying!
I'm also crying!
I'm crying more!
Yes, you are!
I will sleep on the couch!
OK!
Now I will sleep on my friend's couch!
Fine!
I am taking many of my possessions with me!
That is true! I can see by the size of your bag!
You have good deductive reasoning.
The rest of your reasoning sucks!

THE AFTERMATH: PRACTICAL CONSIDERATIONS

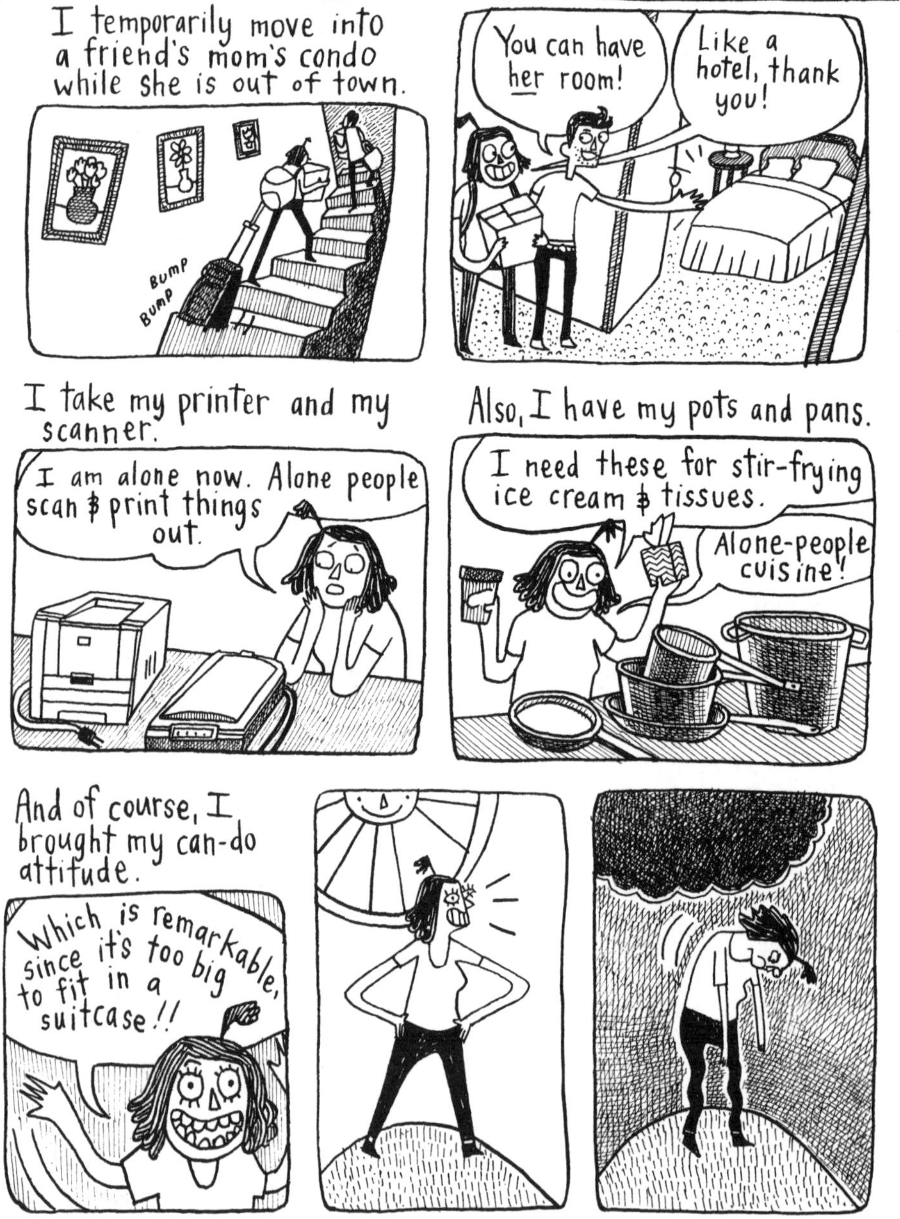

I temporarily move into a friend's mom's condo while she is out of town.
BUMP
BUMP
You can have her room!
Like a hotel, thank you!
I take my printer and my scanner.
I am alone now. Alone people scan & print things out.
Also, I have my pots and pans.
I need these for stir-frying ice cream & tissues.
Alone-people cuisine!
And of course, I brought my can-do attitude.
Which is remarkable, since it's too big to fit in a suitcase!!

Really, though, things are fine. The place I'm crashing is super close to work.

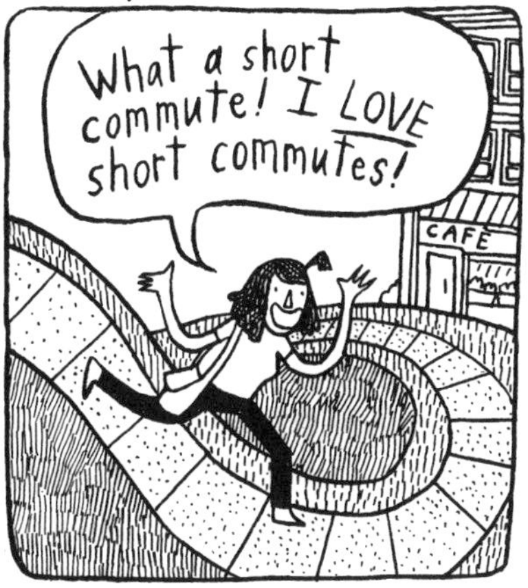
What a short commute! I LOVE short commutes!
CAFÉ

By some WEIRD coincidence, I can't eat or sleep.

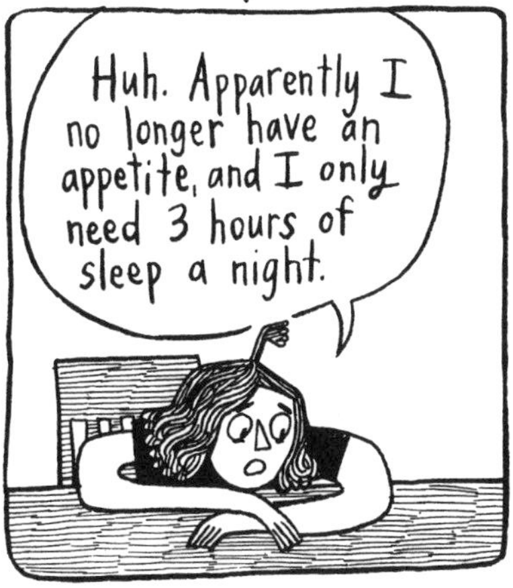
Huh. Apparently I no longer have an appetite, and I only need 3 hours of sleep a night.

I refuse to believe it's because I'm upset about a stupid breakup.

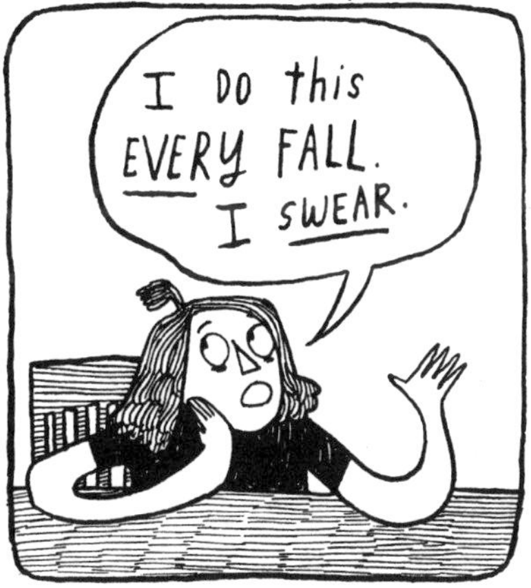
I DO this EVERY FALL. I SWEAR.

Meanwhile, at work, I frequently break down in tears.

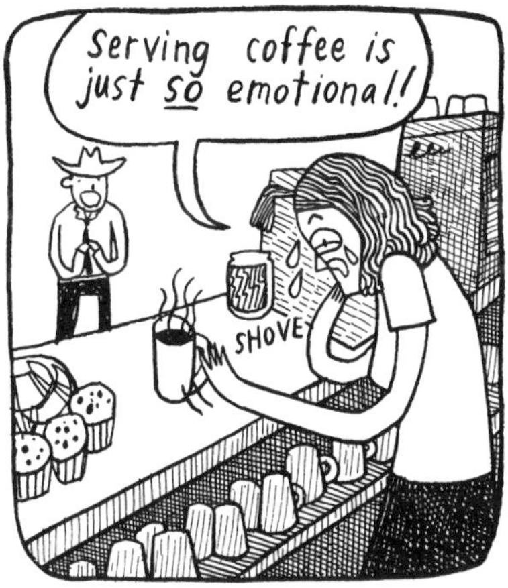
Serving coffee is just SO emotional!
SHOVE

My mind plays ONE version of what my life looks like...
Scorned woman valiently SOARS ONWARD
HER HEART IS HEAVY, BUT HER STEPS ARE LIGHT!
while Reality troops on.
BLUBBERING BETSY
BUH BUH
BUH BUH BAAAAH
SHE NEEDS MORE THAN TISSUES FOR HER ISSUES!
THE SPIRIT OF DENIAL
THE CRUISE THAT TAKES YOU FROM LOVERS LANE to SLEEPING SOLO!
DISEMBARK AT YOUR LEISURE!

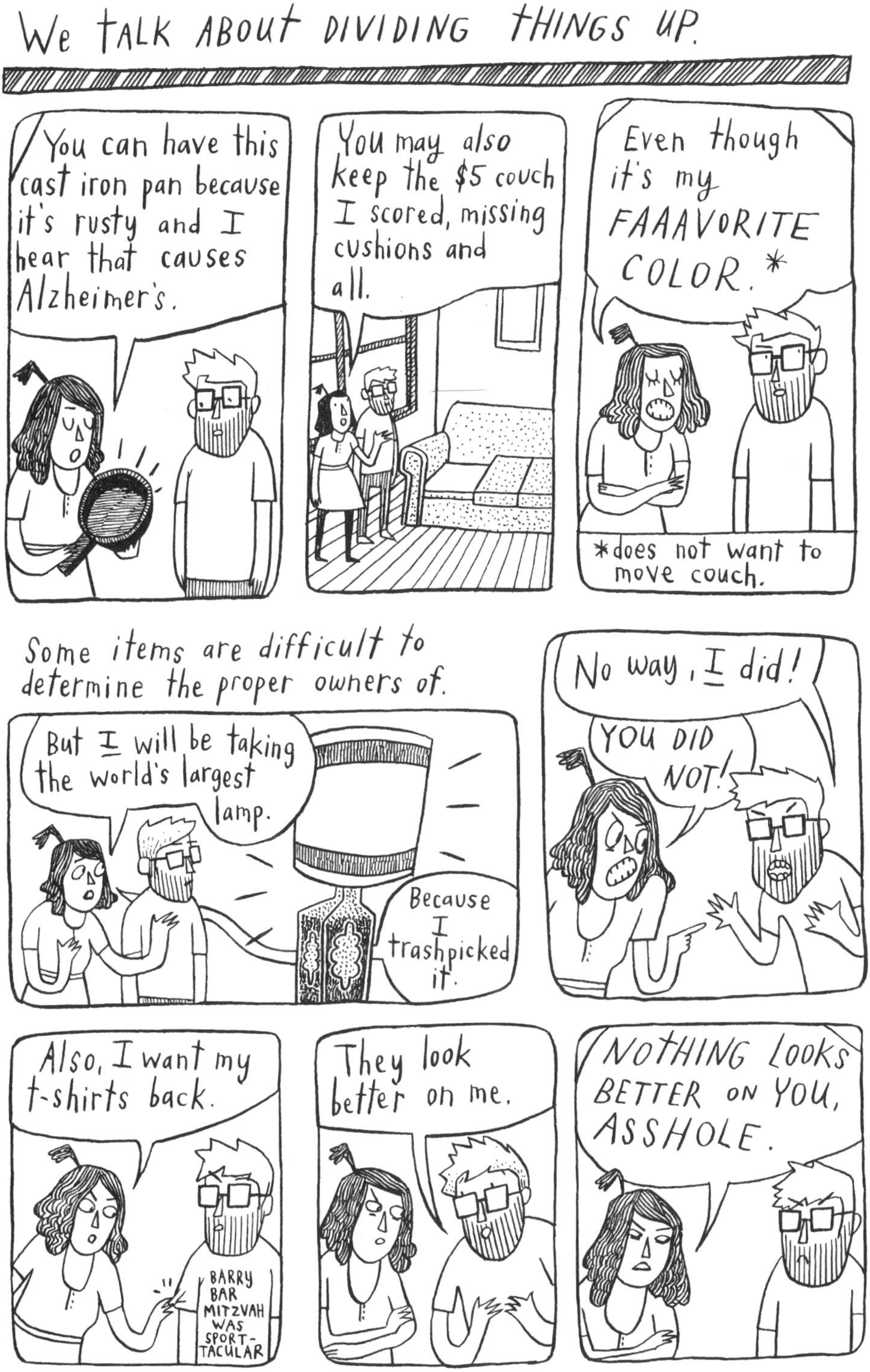
We talk about dividing things up.
You can have this cast iron pan because it's rusty and I hear that causes Alzheimer's.
You may also keep the $5 couch I scored, missing cushions and all.
Even though it's my FAAAVORITE COLOR.*
*does not want to move couch.
Some items are difficult to determine the proper owners of.
But I will be taking the world's largest lamp.
Because I trashpicked it.
No way, I did!
YOU DID NOT!
Also, I want my t-shirts back.
BARRY BAR MITZVAH WAS SPORT-TACULAR
They look better on me.
NOTHING LOOKS BETTER ON YOU, ASSHOLE.

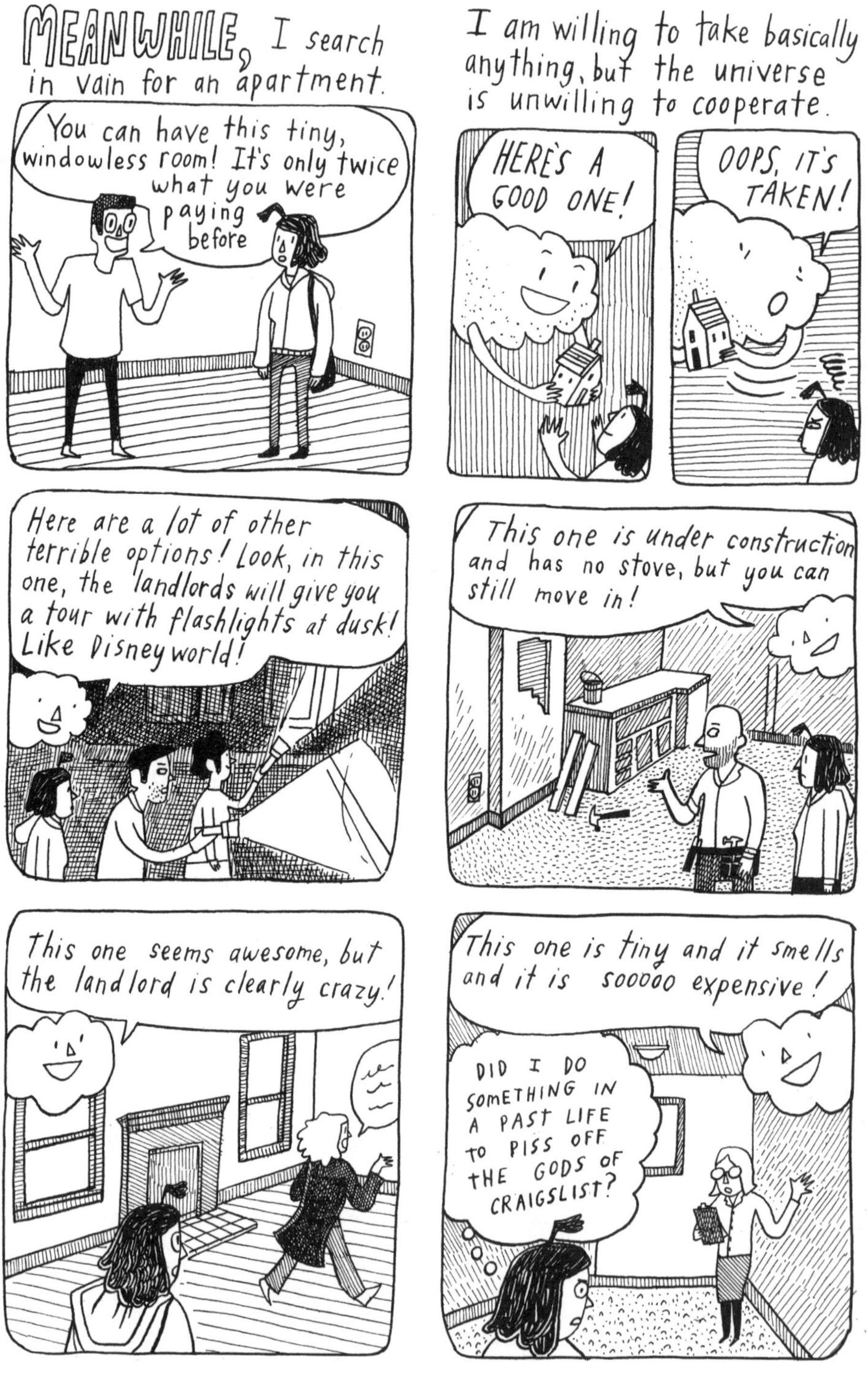
MEANWHILE, I search in vain for an apartment.
You can have this tiny, windowless room! It's only twice what you were paying before
I am willing to take basically anything, but the universe is unwilling to cooperate.
HERE'S A GOOD ONE!
OOPS, IT'S TAKEN!
Here are a lot of other terrible options! Look, in this one, the landlords will give you a tour with flashlights at dusk! Like Disney world!
This one is under construction and has no stove, but you can still move in!
This one seems awesome, but the landlord is clearly crazy!
This one is tiny and it smells and it is sooooo expensive!
DID I DO SOMETHING IN A PAST LIFE TO PISS OFF THE GODS OF CRAIGSLIST?

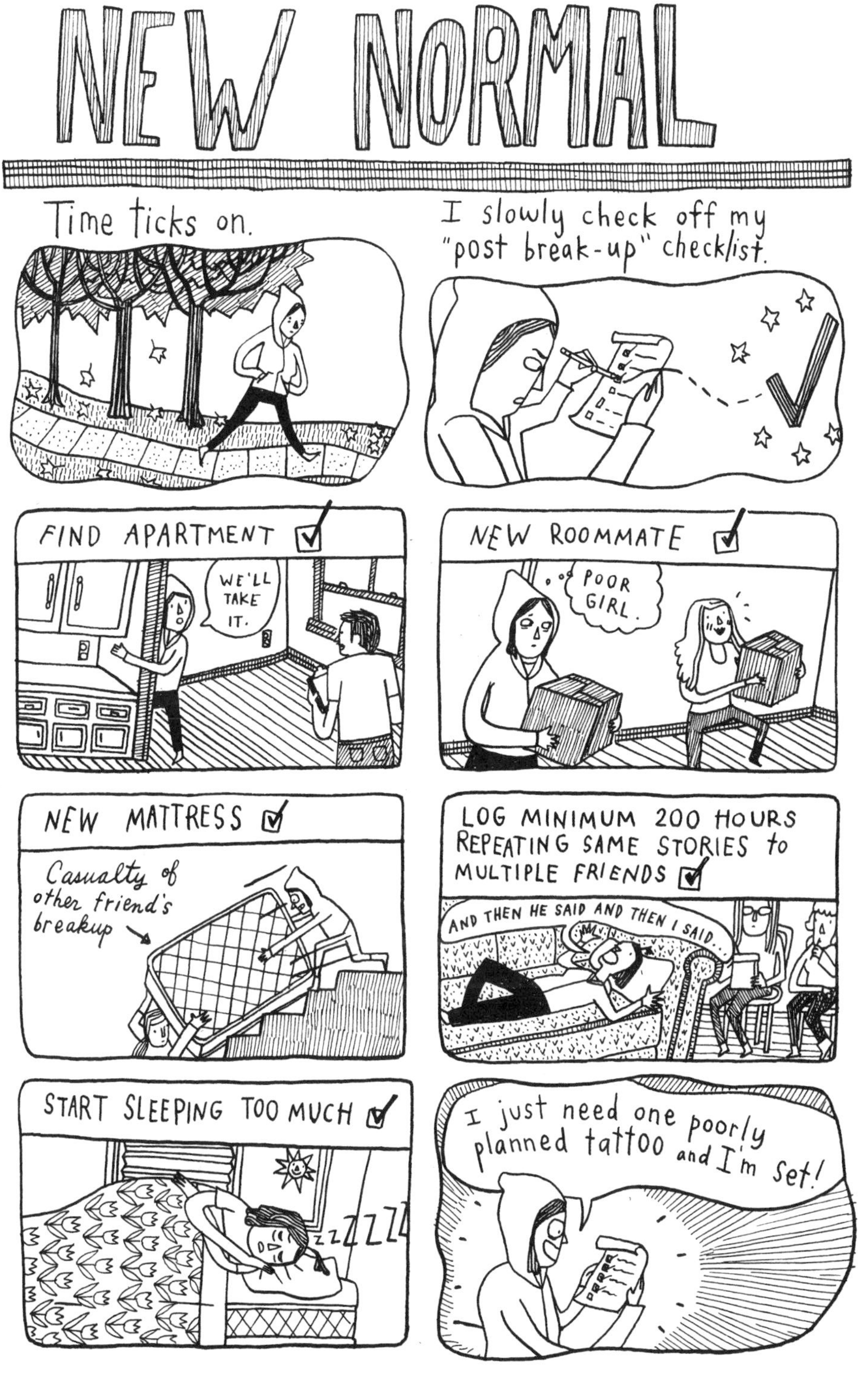
NEW NORMAL
Time ticks on.
I slowly check off my "post break-up" checklist.
FIND APARTMENT
WE'LL TAKE IT.
NEW ROOMMATE
POOR GIRL.
NEW MATTRESS
Casualty of other friend's breakup
LOG MINIMUM 200 HOURS REPEATING SAME STORIES to MULTIPLE FRIENDS
AND THEN HE SAID AND THEN I SAID...
START SLEEPING TOO MUCH
zzZZZZ
I just need one poorly planned tattoo and I'm set!

Life assumes a "new normal."

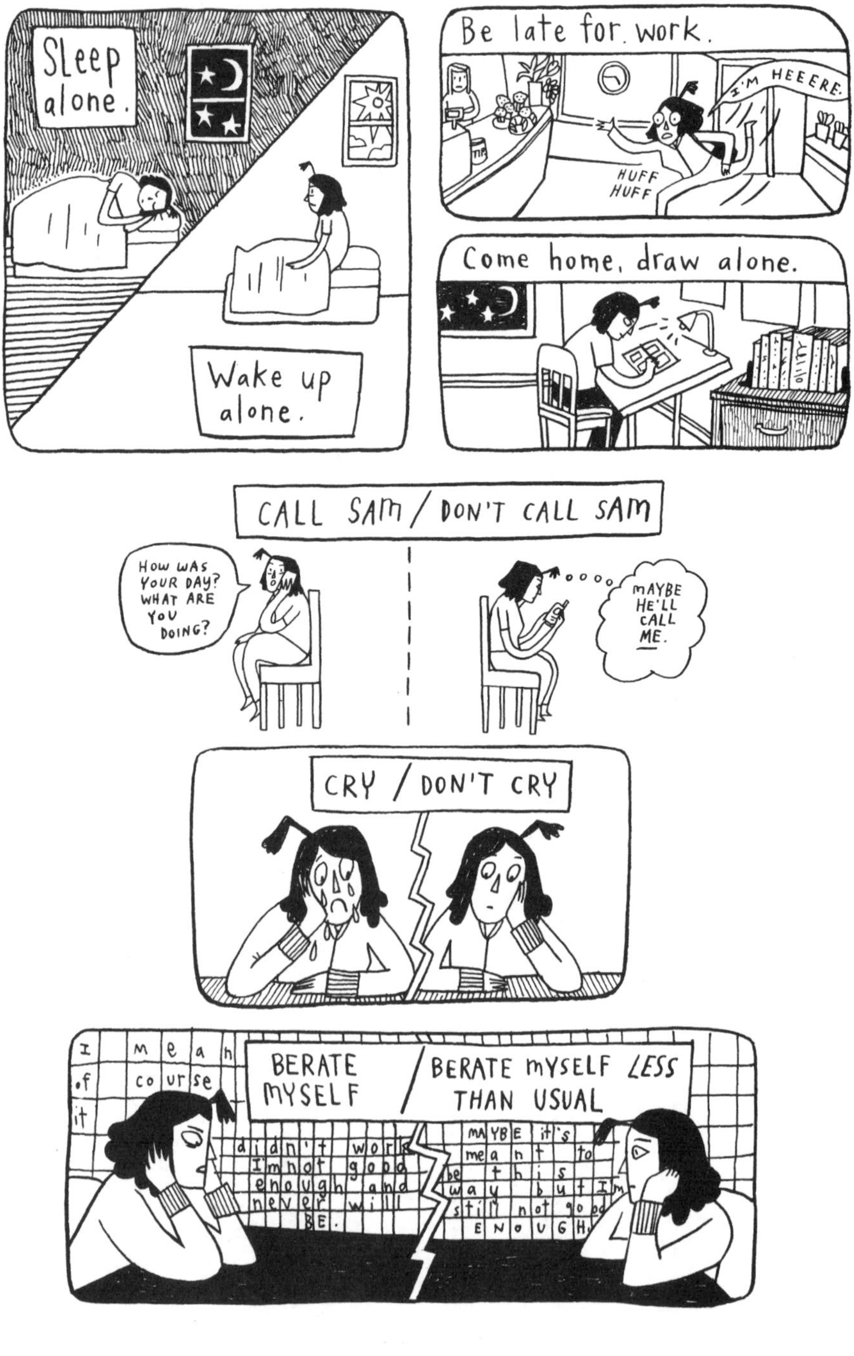
Sleep alone.
Wake up alone.
Be late for work.
I'M HEEERE.
HUFF HUFF
TIP
Come home, draw alone.
CALL SAM / DON'T CALL SAM
HOW WAS YOUR DAY? WHAT ARE YOU DOING?
MAYBE HE'LL CALL ME.
CRY / DON'T CRY
BERATE MYSELF / BERATE MYSELF LESS THAN USUAL
I mean of course it didn't work I'm not good enough and never will BE.
MAYBE it's meant to be this way but I'm still not good ENOUGH.

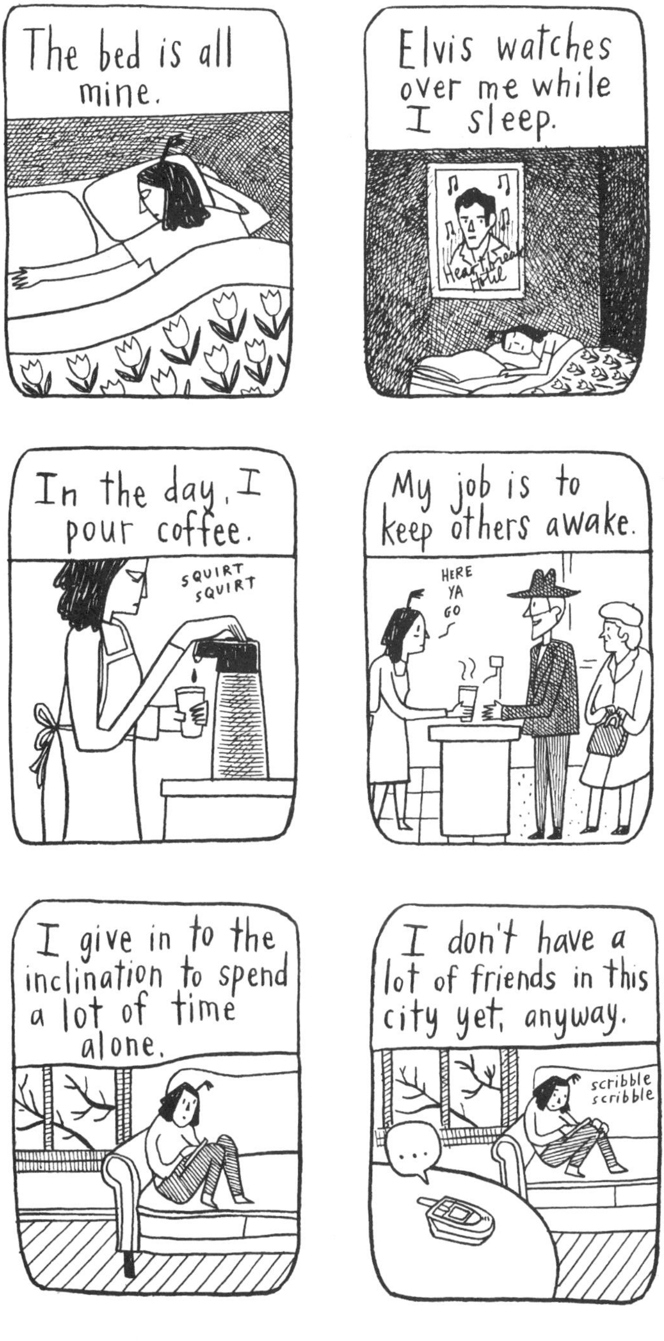
The bed is all mine.
Elvis watches over me while I sleep.
Heartbreak Hotel
In the day, I pour coffee.
SQUIRT SQUIRT
My job is to keep others awake.
HERE YA GO
I give in to the inclination to spend a lot of time alone.
I don't have a lot of friends in this city yet, anyway.
...
scribble scribble

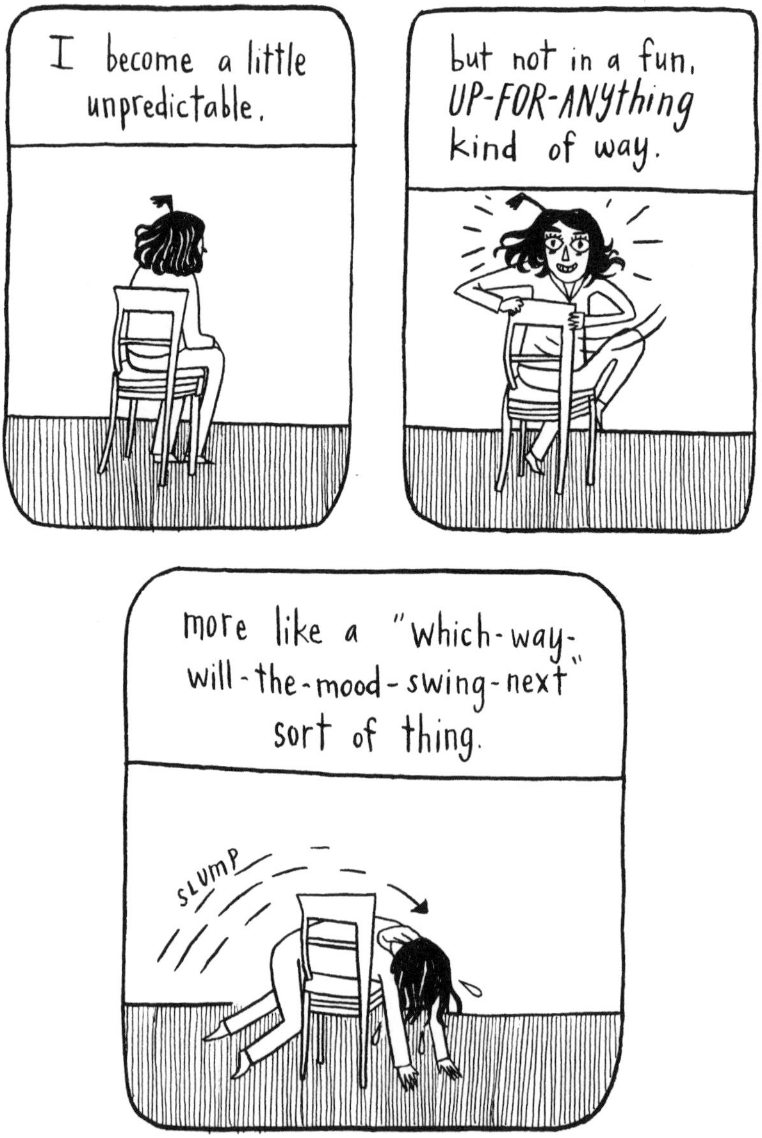
I become a little unpredictable.
but not in a fun, UP-FOR-ANYthing kind of way.
more like a "which-way-will-the-mood-swing-next" sort of thing.
SLUMP

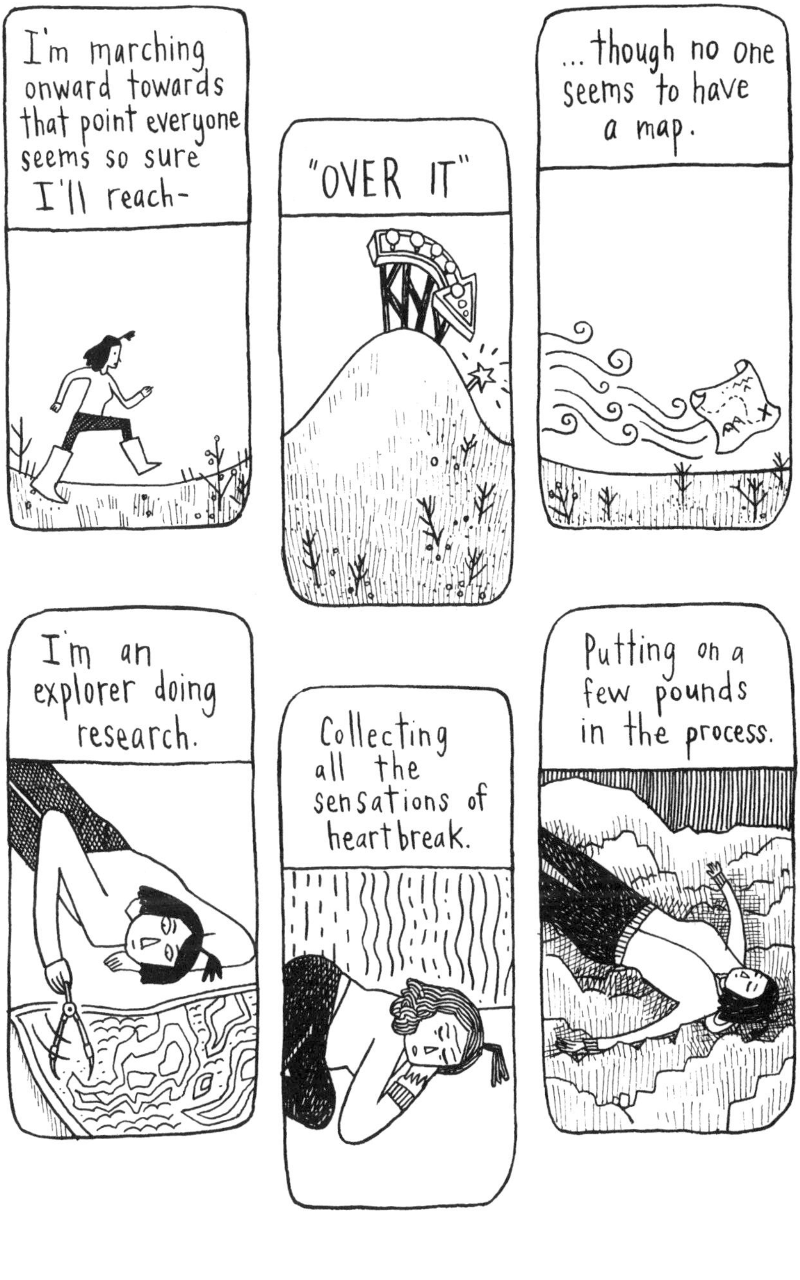
I'm marching onward towards that point everyone seems so sure I'll reach-
"OVER IT"
...though no one seems to have a map.
I'm an explorer doing research.
Collecting all the sensations of heartbreak.
Putting on a few pounds in the process.

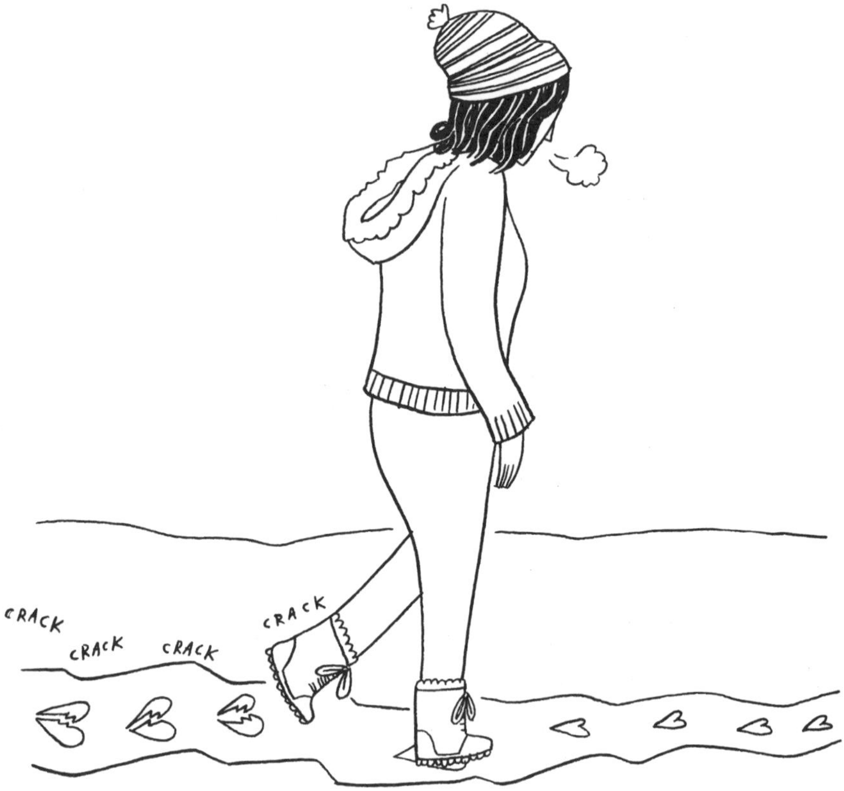
CRACK
CRACK
CRACK
CRACK

Every step is heavy
when you feel sorry
for yourself.

INTERMISSION

Of course, I did what any smart girl does, and leapt into the arms of another person.

CATCH ME!
I'M A MESS!

I convinced myself that this was neither a fling, nor a rebound.

I know the timing's weird, but what we have is REAL!!

This relationship had the endurance of a crudely made paper airplane.

SHOWING PROMISE
SEEMS OK!
VERY NOT OK
SHIT.

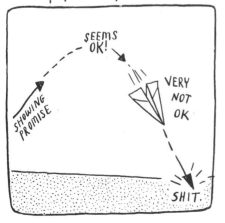

The kind that spontaneously disintegrates within six weeks.

DIAGNOSIS: total ENGINE FAILURE.
Did you REALLY not see that coming?

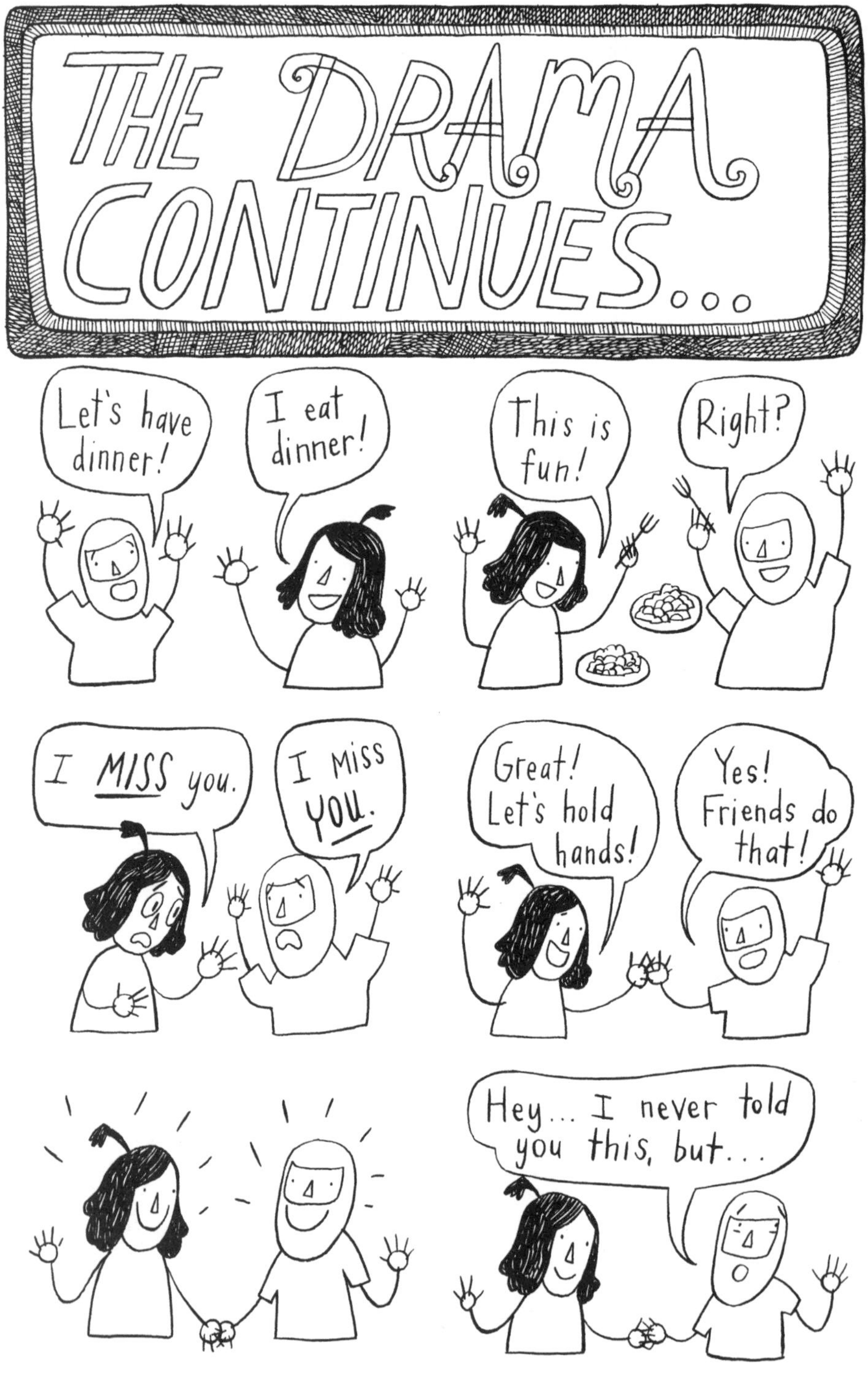
THE DRAMA CONTINUES...
Let's have dinner!
I eat dinner!
This is fun!
Right?
I MISS you.
I miss YOU.
Great! Let's hold hands!
Yes! Friends do that!
Hey... I never told you this, but...

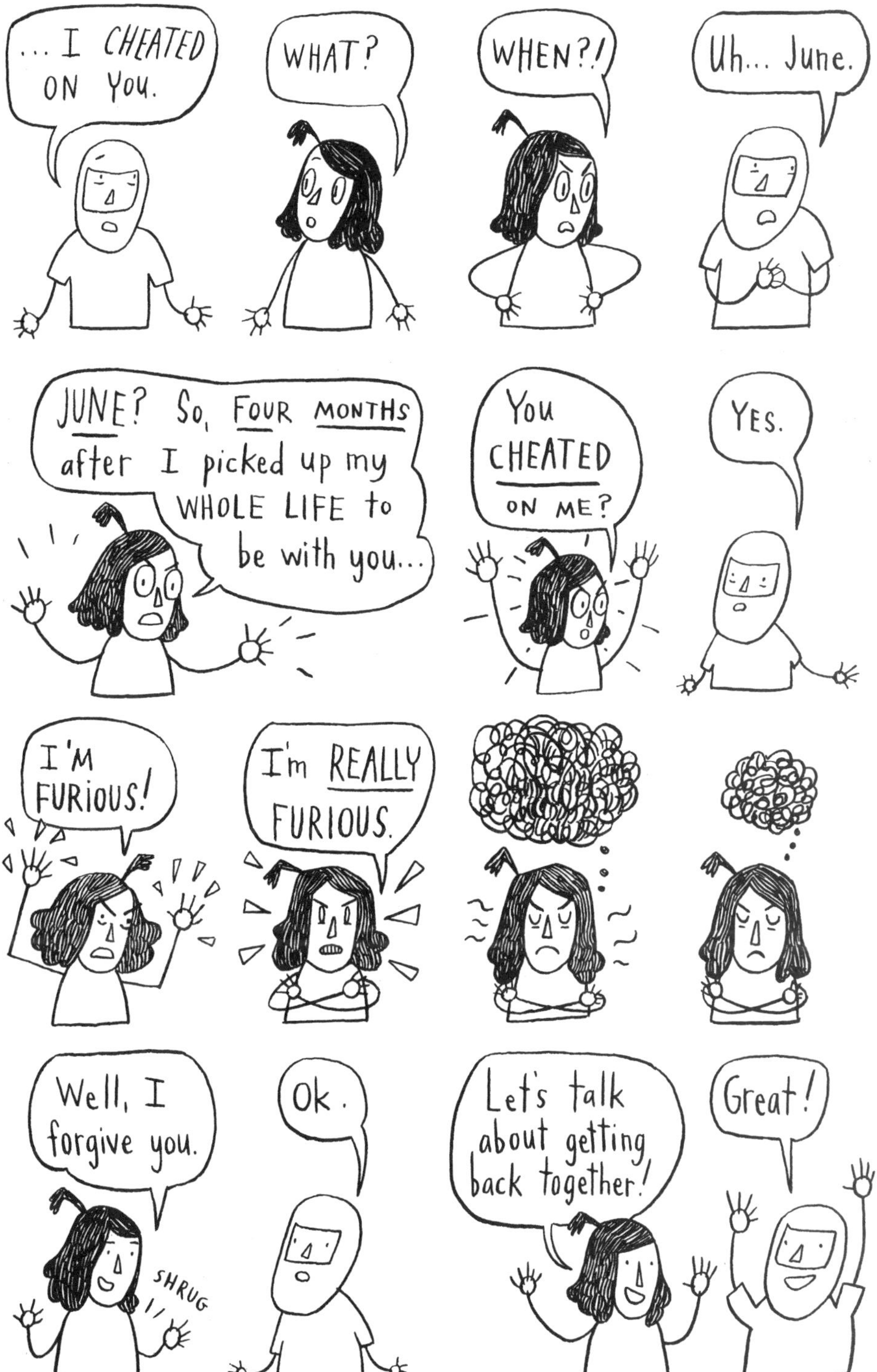
...I CHEATED ON YOU.
WHAT?
WHEN?!
Uh... June.
JUNE? So, FOUR MONTHS after I picked up my WHOLE LIFE to be with you...
You CHEATED ON ME?
YES.
I'M FURIOUS!
I'm REALLY FURIOUS.
Well, I forgive you.
SHRUG
Ok.
Let's talk about getting back together!
Great!

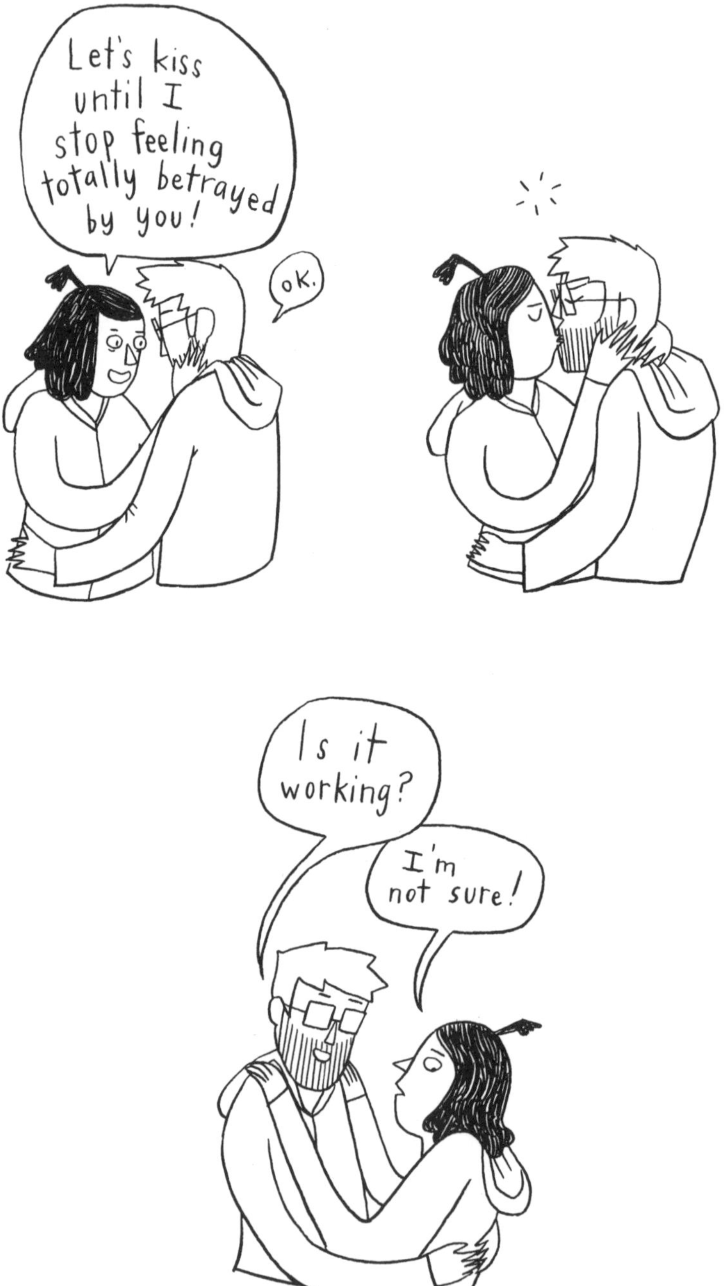
Let's kiss until I stop feeling totally betrayed by you!
ok.
Is it working?
I'm not sure!

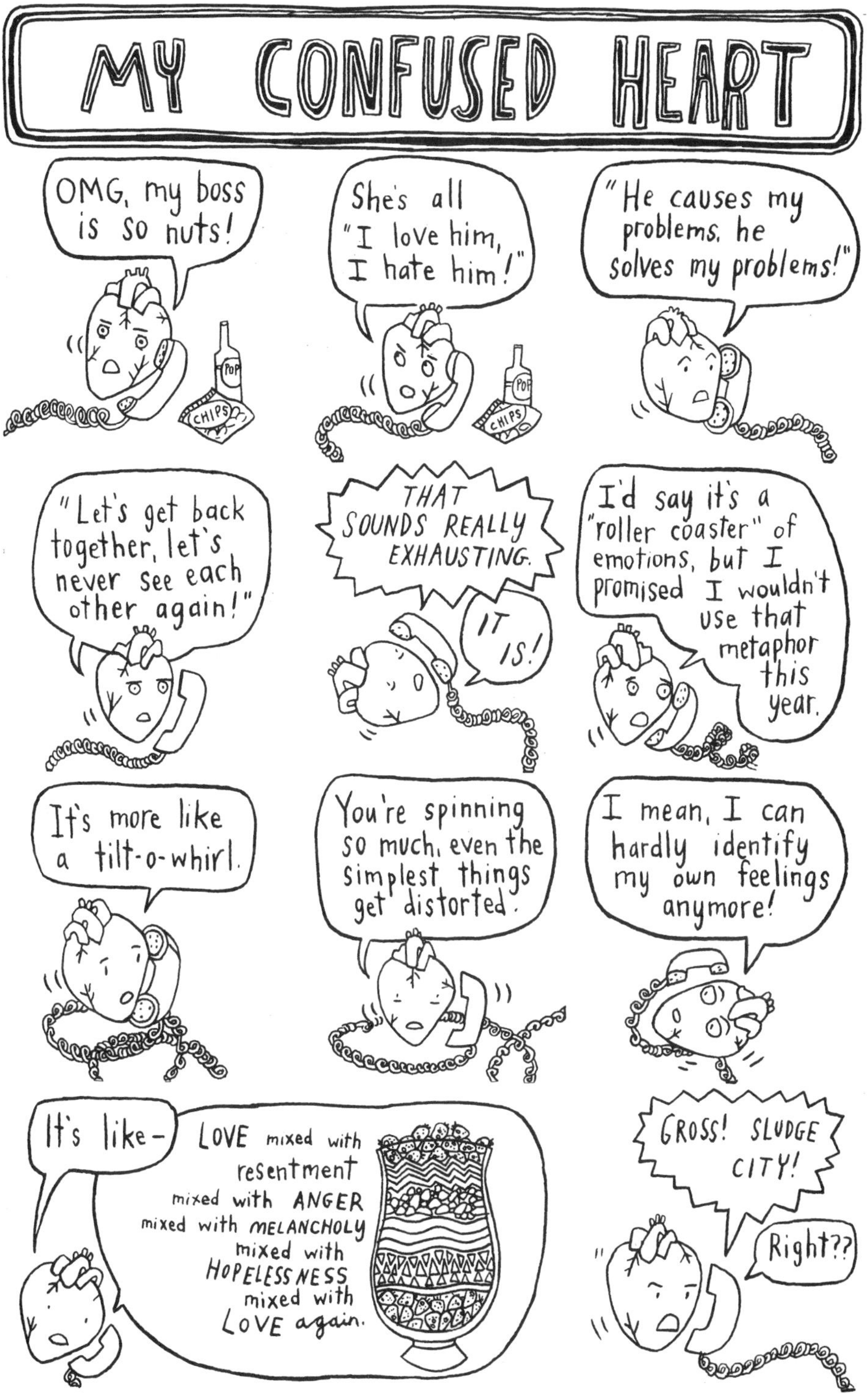
MY CONFUSED HEART
OMG, my boss is so nuts!
POP
CHIPS
She's all "I love him, I hate him!"
POP
CHIPS
"He causes my problems, he solves my problems!"
"Let's get back together, let's never see each other again!"
THAT SOUNDS REALLY EXHAUSTING.
IT IS!
I'd say it's a "roller coaster" of emotions, but I promised I wouldn't use that metaphor this year.
It's more like a tilt-o-whirl.
You're spinning so much, even the simplest things get distorted.
I mean, I can hardly identify my own feelings anymore!
It's like–
LOVE mixed with resentment mixed with ANGER mixed with MELANCHOLY mixed with HOPELESSNESS mixed with LOVE again.
GROSS! SLUDGE CITY!
Right??

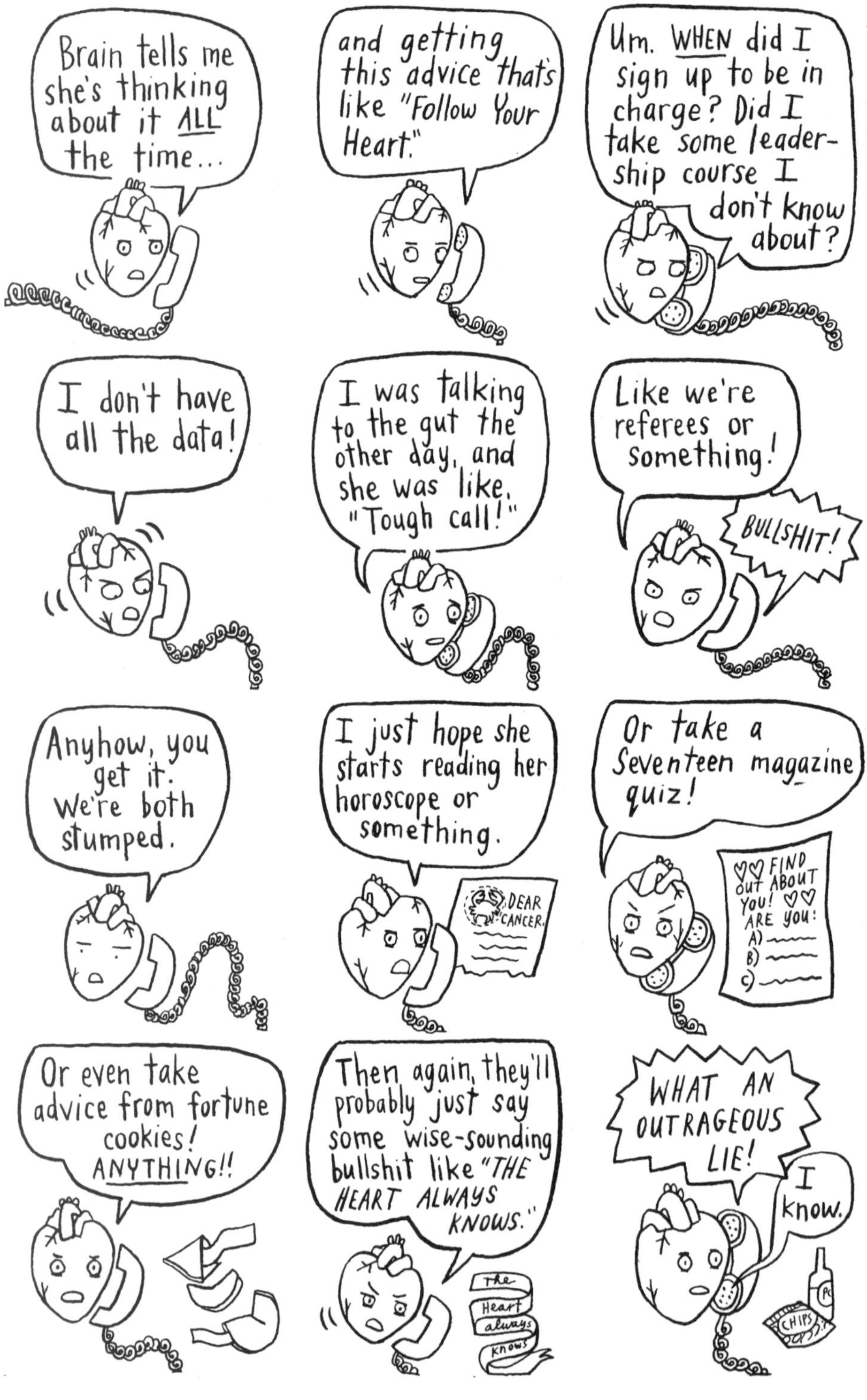
Brain tells me she's thinking about it ALL the time...
and getting this advice that's like "Follow Your Heart."
Um. WHEN did I sign up to be in charge? Did I take some leader-ship course I don't know about?
I don't have all the data!
I was talking to the gut the other day, and she was like, "Tough call!"
Like we're referees or something!
BULLSHIT!
Anyhow, you get it. We're both stumped.
I just hope she starts reading her horoscope or something.
DEAR CANCER
Or take a Seventeen magazine quiz!
FIND OUT ABOUT YOU!
ARE YOU:
A)
B)
C)
Or even take advice from fortune cookies! ANYTHING!!
Then again, they'll probably just say some wise-sounding bullshit like "THE HEART ALWAYS KNOWS."
The Heart always knows
WHAT AN OUTRAGEOUS LIE!
I know.
CHIPS

RESOLUTIONS

Christmas had come and gone.
In the spirit of the New Year,
I decided a fresh start was required.

My resolution is for us to never, ever get back together.
And to remember to water my plants, for once!
Alright, I'll talk to you later.

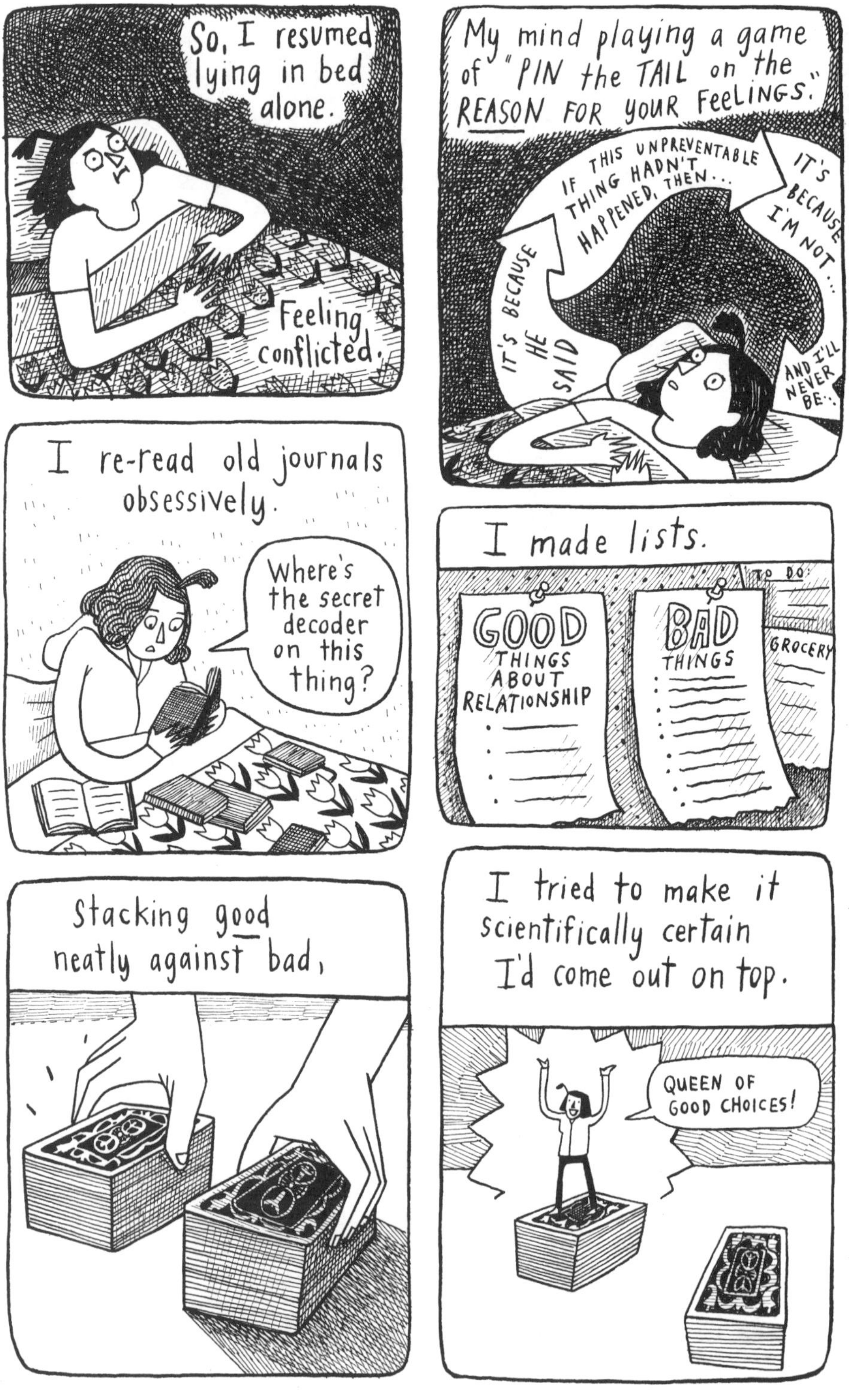
So, I resumed lying in bed alone.
Feeling conflicted.
My mind playing a game of "PIN the TAIL on the REASON FOR YOUR FeeLINGS."
IT'S BECAUSE HE SAID
IF THIS UNPREVENTABLE THING HADN'T HAPPENED, THEN...
IT'S BECAUSE I'M NOT...
AND I'LL NEVER BE...
I re-read old journals obsessively.
Where's the secret decoder on this thing?
I made lists.
GOOD THINGS ABOUT RELATIONSHIP
BAD THINGS
TO DO:
GROCERY
Stacking good neatly against bad,
I tried to make it scientifically certain I'd come out on top.
QUEEN OF GOOD CHOICES!

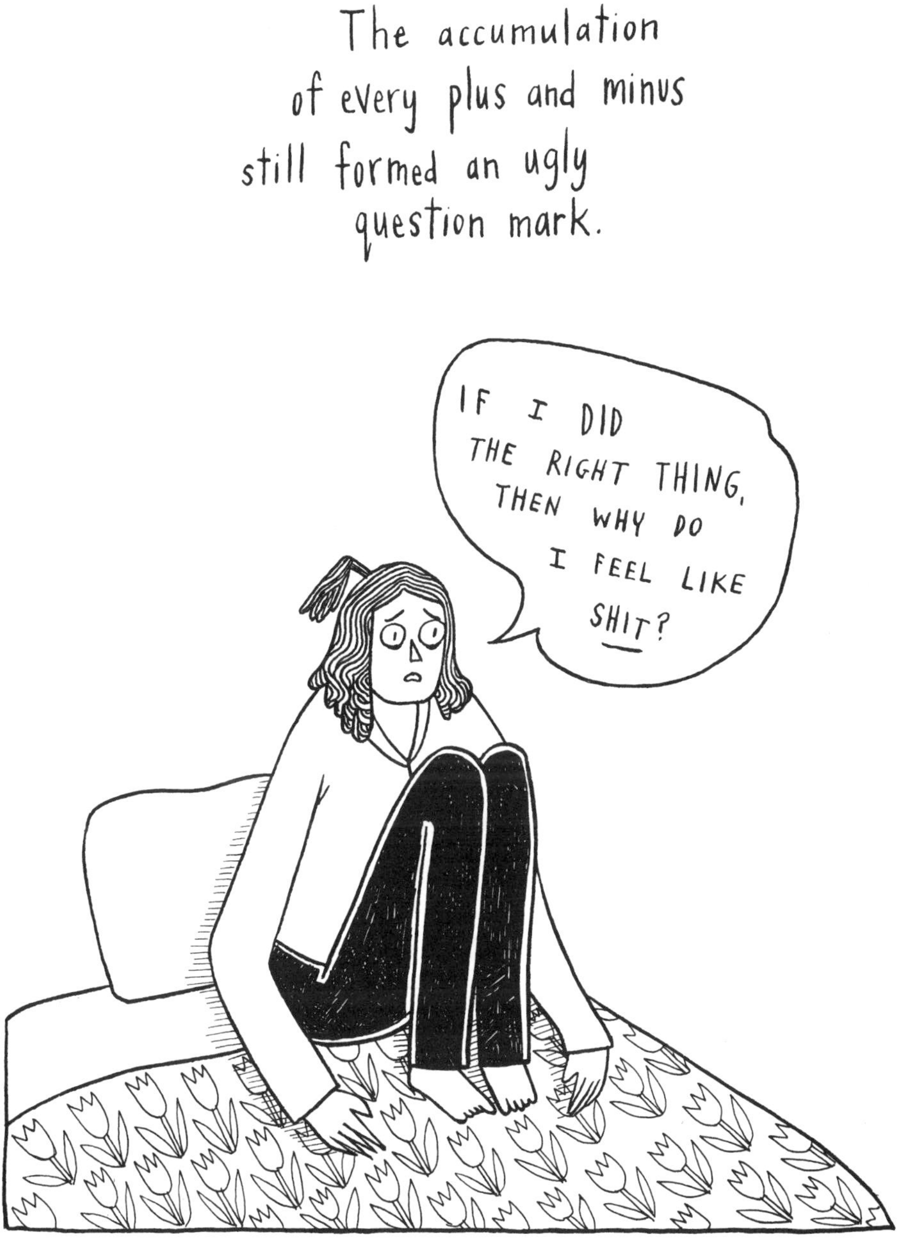
The accumulation of every plus and minus still formed an ugly question mark.
IF I DID THE RIGHT THING, THEN WHY DO I FEEL LIKE SHIT?

PART
TWO

· AFTERMATH ·

They should really name relationships after hurricanes.

Why?

Because even after it's over, it continues to affect everything it touched.

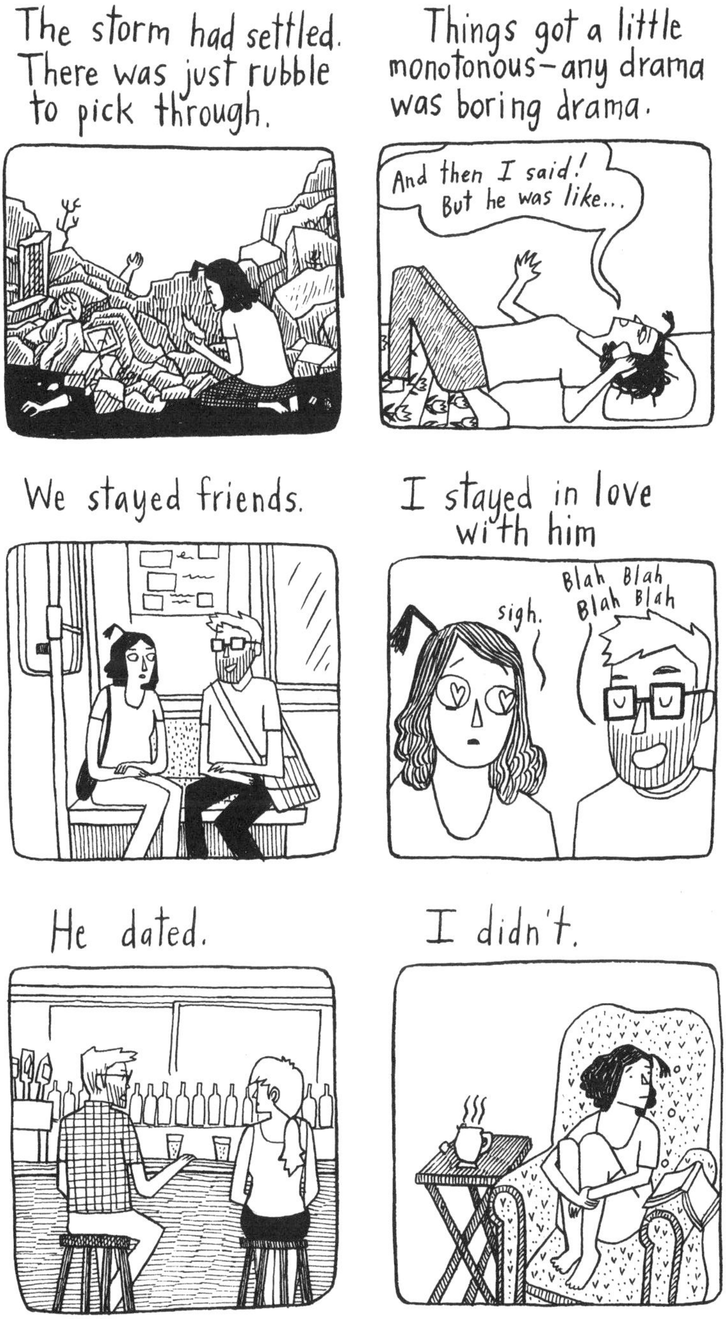
The storm had settled. There was just rubble to pick through.
Things got a little monotonous—any drama was boring drama.
And then I said! But he was like...
We stayed friends.
I stayed in love with him
sigh.
Blah Blah Blah Blah
He dated.
I didn't.

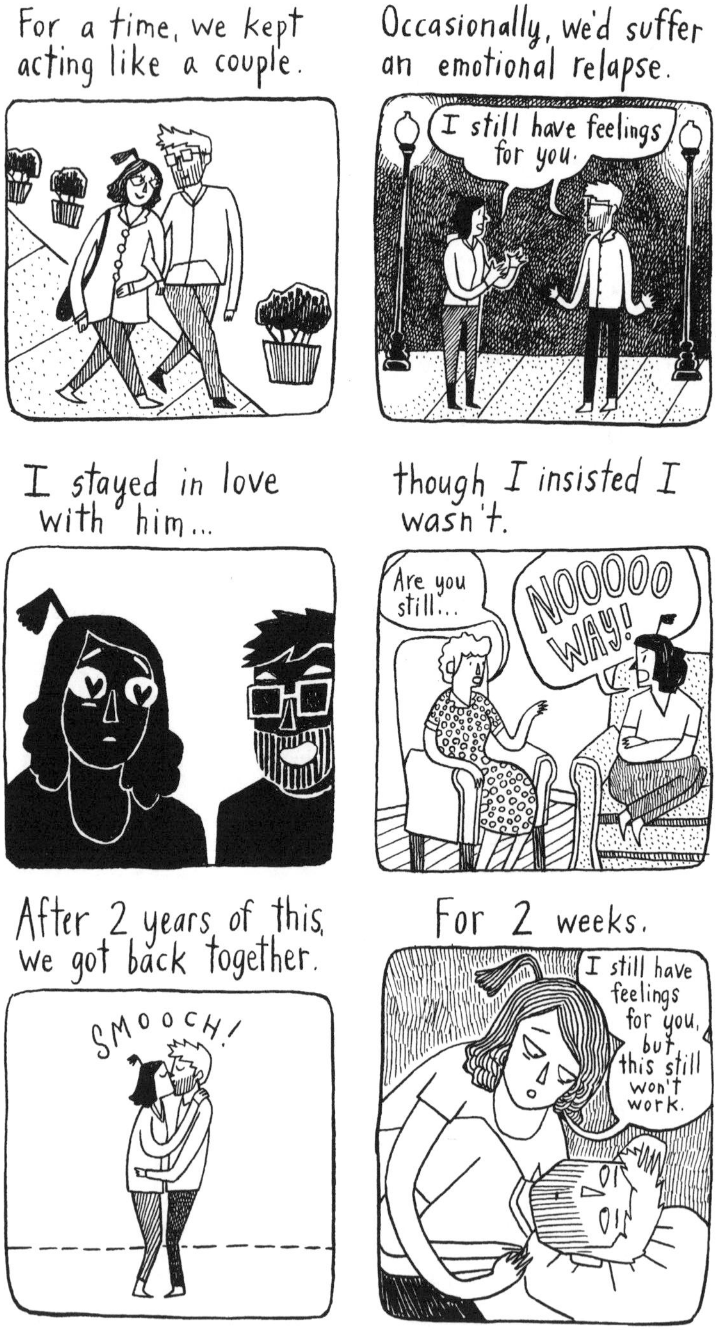
For a time, we kept acting like a couple.
Occasionally, we'd suffer an emotional relapse.
I still have feelings for you.
I stayed in love with him...
though I insisted I wasn't.
Are you still...
NOOOOO WAY!
After 2 years of this, we got back together.
SMOOCH!
For 2 weeks.
I still have feelings for you, but this still won't work.

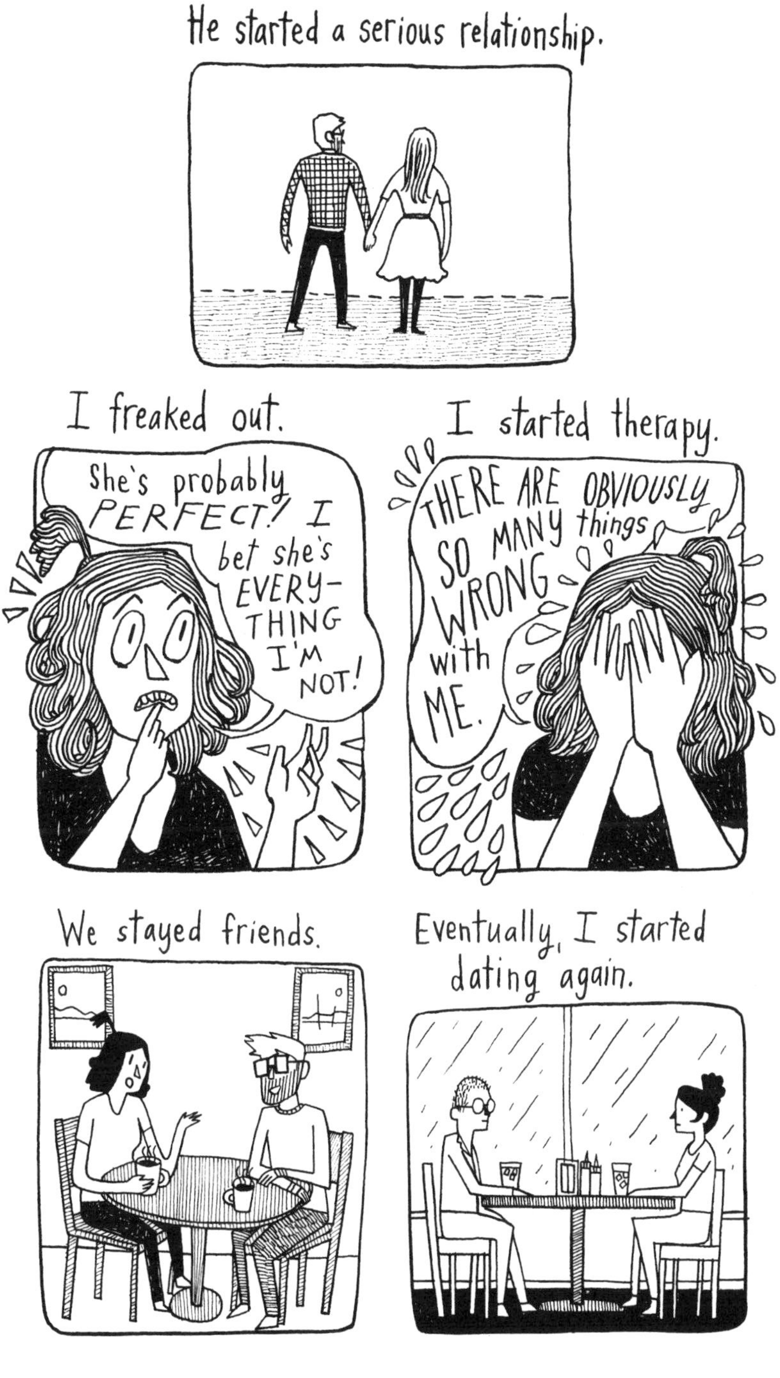
He started a serious relationship.
I freaked out.
She's probably PERFECT! I bet she's EVERYTHING I'M NOT!
I started therapy.
THERE ARE OBVIOUSLY SO MANY things WRONG with ME.
We stayed friends.
Eventually, I started dating again.

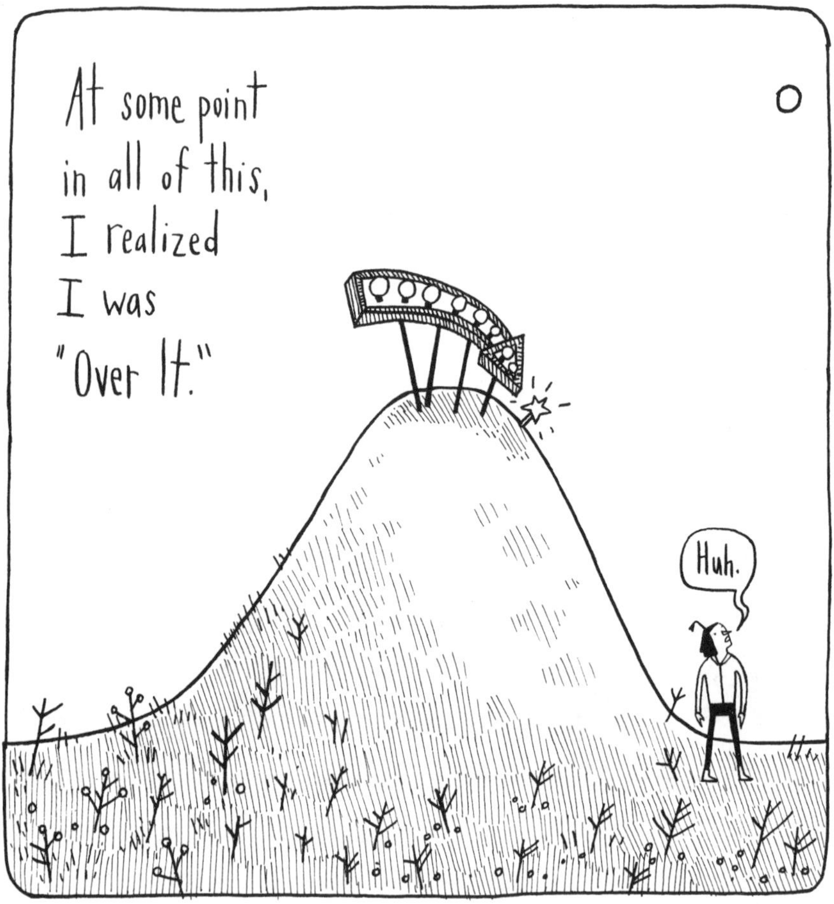
At some point in all of this, I realized I was "Over It."
Huh.

Though, of course, these things never really happen when you want them to.

April
March
February
ANUARY
May
June
July
AUGUS
TICK TOCK
TICK TOCK

Or the way you expect them to.

hmmm.
PULL
PULL
PULL
PULL

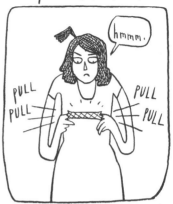

Falling *OUT* of love with someone is sort of like falling *IN* love.

It has a way of happening when you aren't looking.

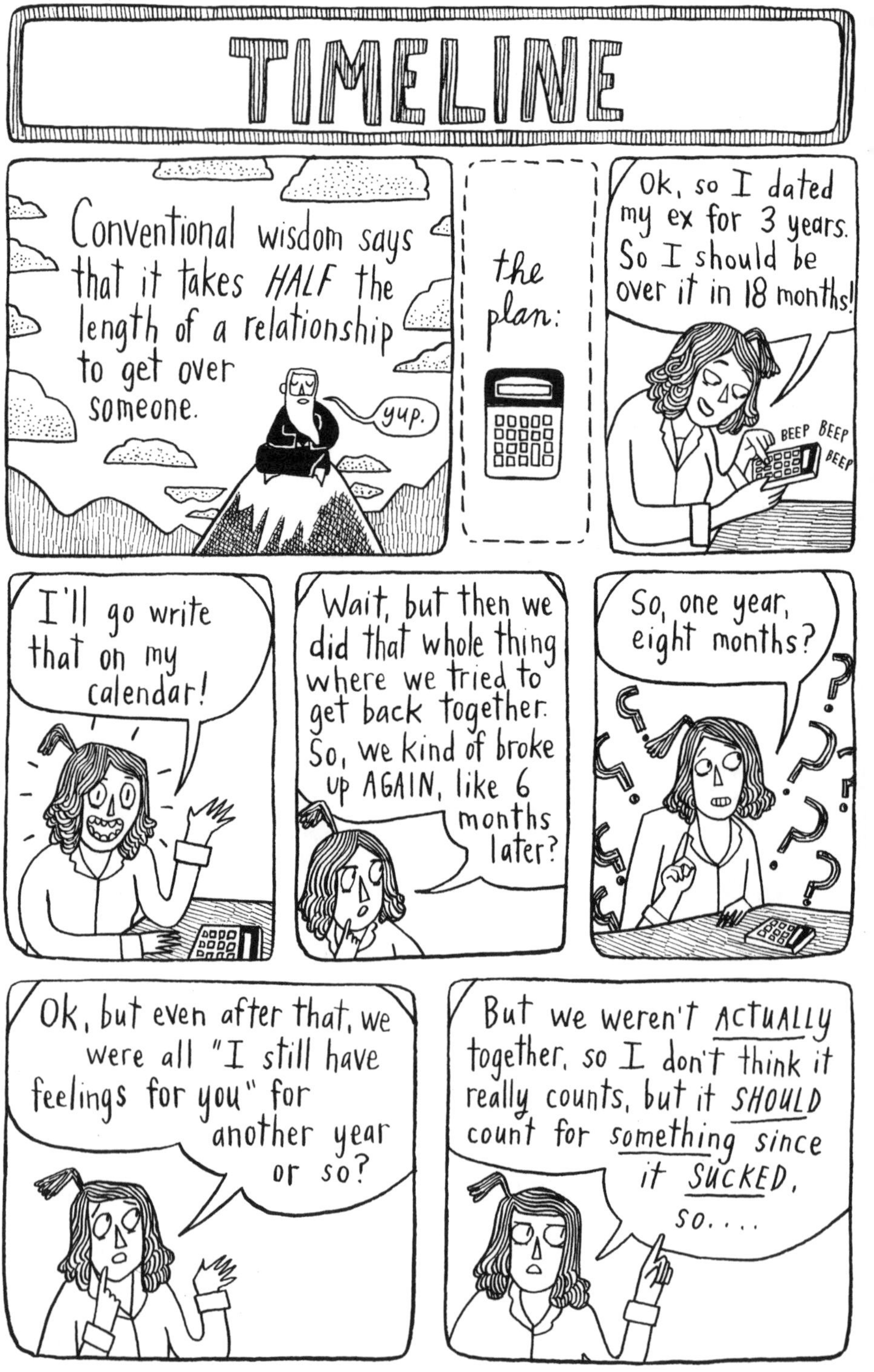
TIMELINE
Conventional wisdom says that it takes HALF the length of a relationship to get over someone.
yup.
the plan:
Ok, so I dated my ex for 3 years. So I should be over it in 18 months!
BEEP BEEP BEEP
I'll go write that on my calendar!
Wait, but then we did that whole thing where we tried to get back together. So, we kind of broke up AGAIN, like 6 months later?
So, one year, eight months?
Ok, but even after that, we were all "I still have feelings for you" for another year or so?
But we weren't ACTUALLY together, so I don't think it really counts, but it SHOULD count for something since it SUCKED, so....

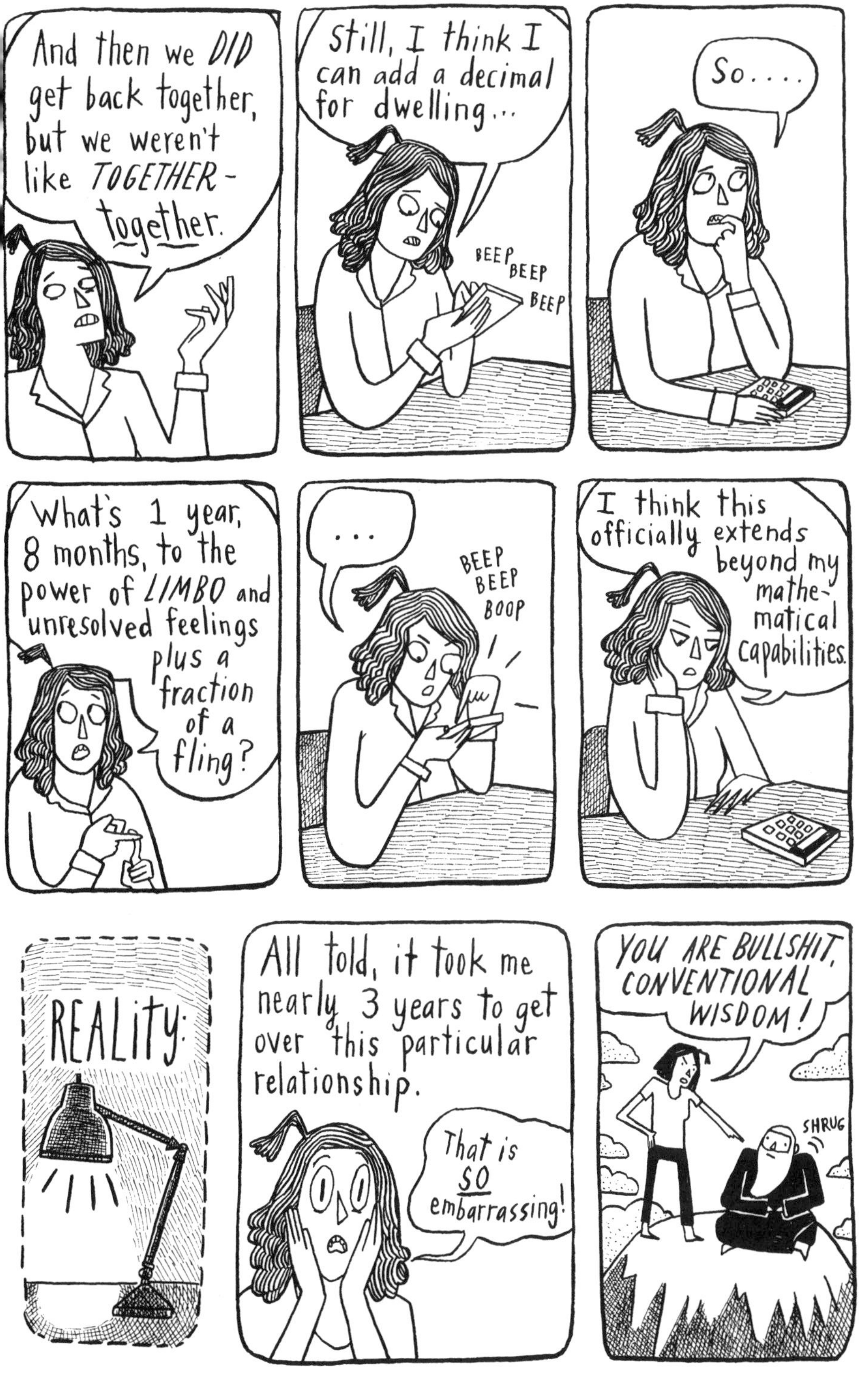

And then we DID get back together, but we weren't like TOGETHER-together.
Still, I think I can add a decimal for dwelling...
BEEP BEEP BEEP
So....
What's 1 year, 8 months, to the power of LIMBO and unresolved feelings plus a fraction of a fling?
...
BEEP BEEP BOOP
I think this officially extends beyond my mathematical capabilities.
REALITY:
All told, it took me nearly 3 years to get over this particular relationship.
That is SO embarrassing!
YOU ARE BULLSHIT, CONVENTIONAL WISDOM!
SHRUG

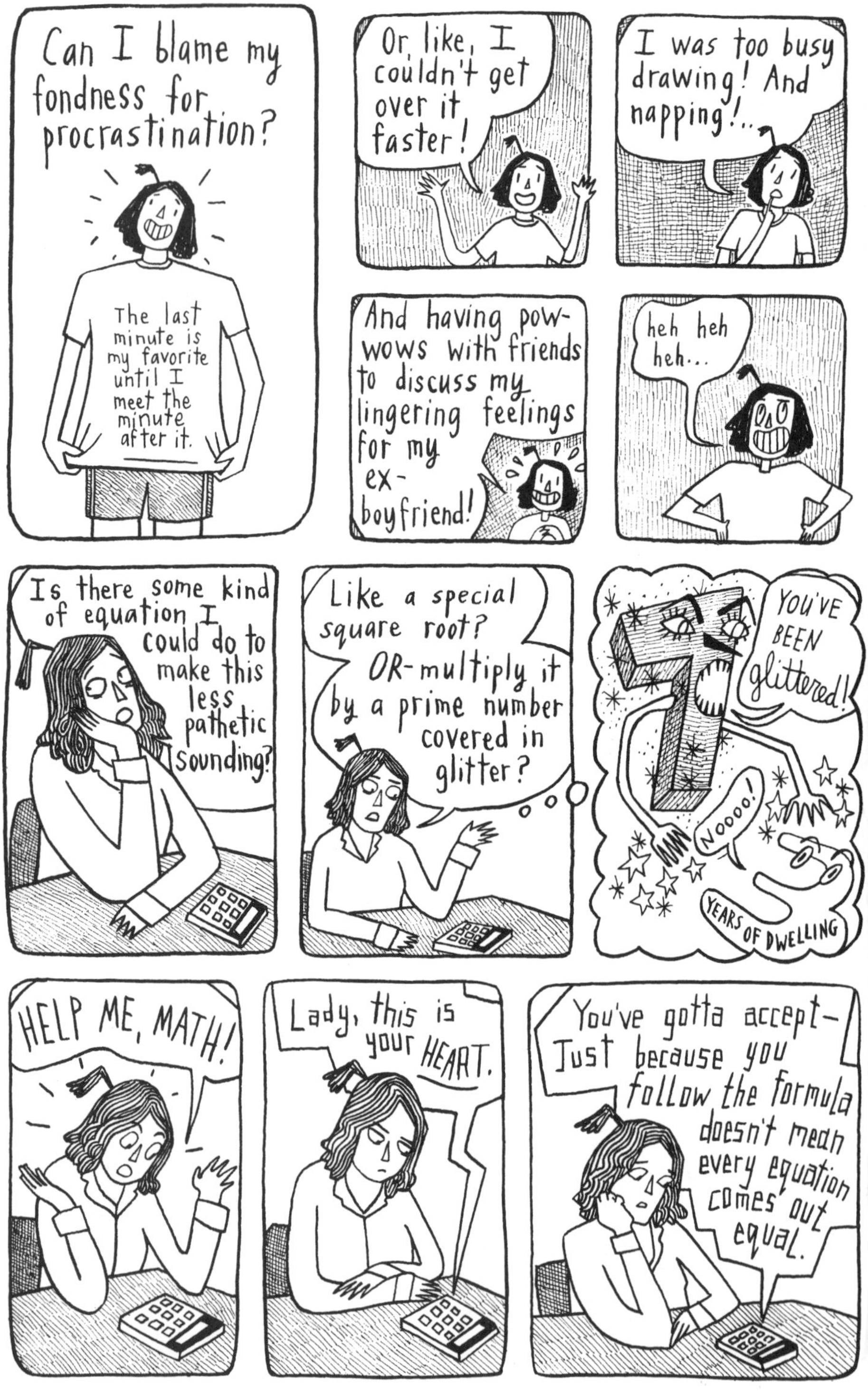
Can I blame my fondness for procrastination?
The last minute is my favorite until I meet the minute after it.
Or, like, I couldn't get over it faster!
I was too busy drawing! And napping!...
And having pow-wows with friends to discuss my lingering feelings for my ex-boyfriend!
heh heh heh...
Is there some kind of equation I could do to make this less pathetic sounding?
Like a special square root? OR-multiply it by a prime number covered in glitter?
YOU'VE BEEN glittered!
Noooo!
YEARS OF DWELLING
HELP ME, MATH!
Lady, this is your HEART.
You've gotta accept- Just because you follow the formula doesn't mean every equation comes out equal.

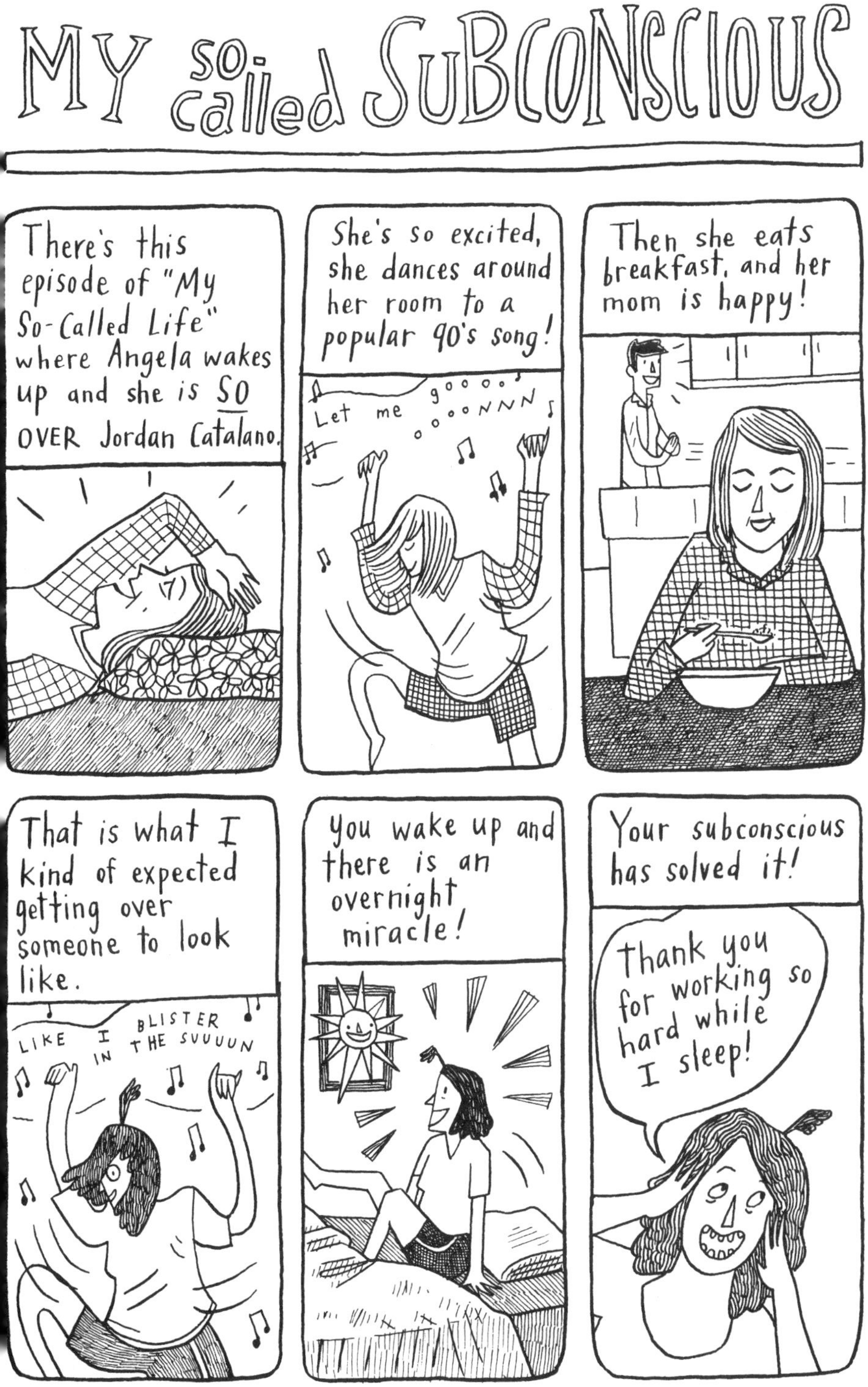
MY SO-called SUBCONSCIOUS
There's this episode of "My So-Called Life" where Angela wakes up and she is SO OVER Jordan Catalano.
(?)
She's so excited, she dances around her room to a popular 90's song!
Let me gooooo oooooNNN
Then she eats breakfast, and her mom is happy!
That is what I kind of expected getting over someone to look like.
LIKE I BLISTER IN THE SUUUUN
You wake up and there is an overnight miracle!
Your subconscious has solved it!
Thank you for working so hard while I sleep!

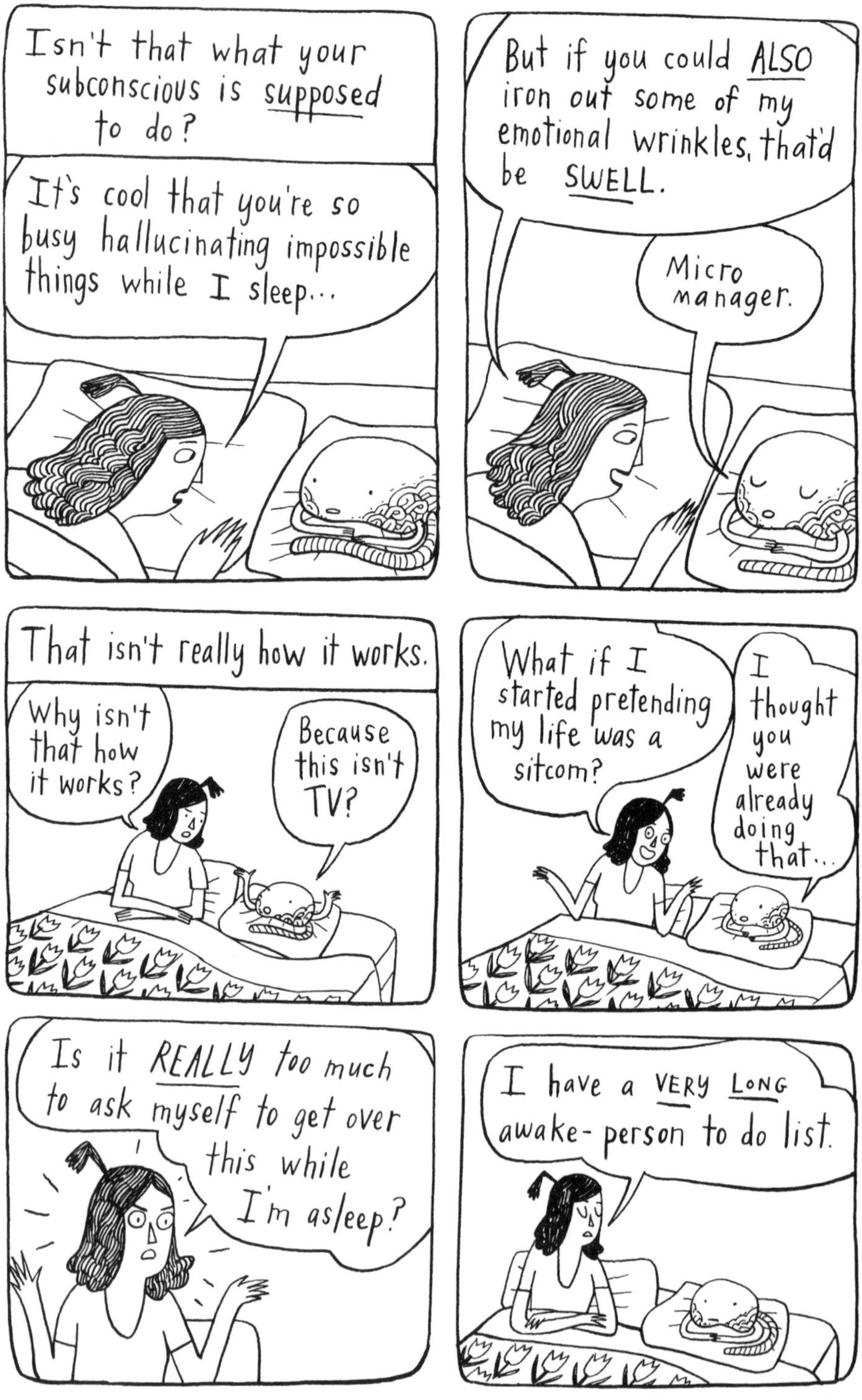
Isn't that what your subconscious is supposed to do?
It's cool that you're so busy hallucinating impossible things while I sleep...
But if you could ALSO iron out some of my emotional wrinkles, that'd be SWELL.
Micro manager.
That isn't really how it works.
Why isn't that how it works?
Because this isn't TV?
What if I started pretending my life was a sitcom?
I thought you were already doing that...
Is it REALLY too much to ask myself to get over this while I'm asleep?
I have a VERY LONG awake-person to do list.

Why CAN'T you just sleep off heartache like any other *garden variety* weariness?

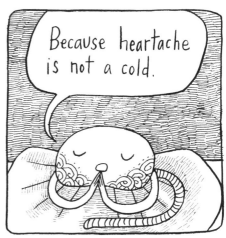

Because heartache is not a cold.

It's an inflammation you keep feeding.

Reliving old memories

Talking to your ex

Telling yourself you'll be alone forever

Etc.

I really think you need to put more work into getting over this while you are awake.

It'd also be great if you got up on time for work once in a while.

Micro manager.

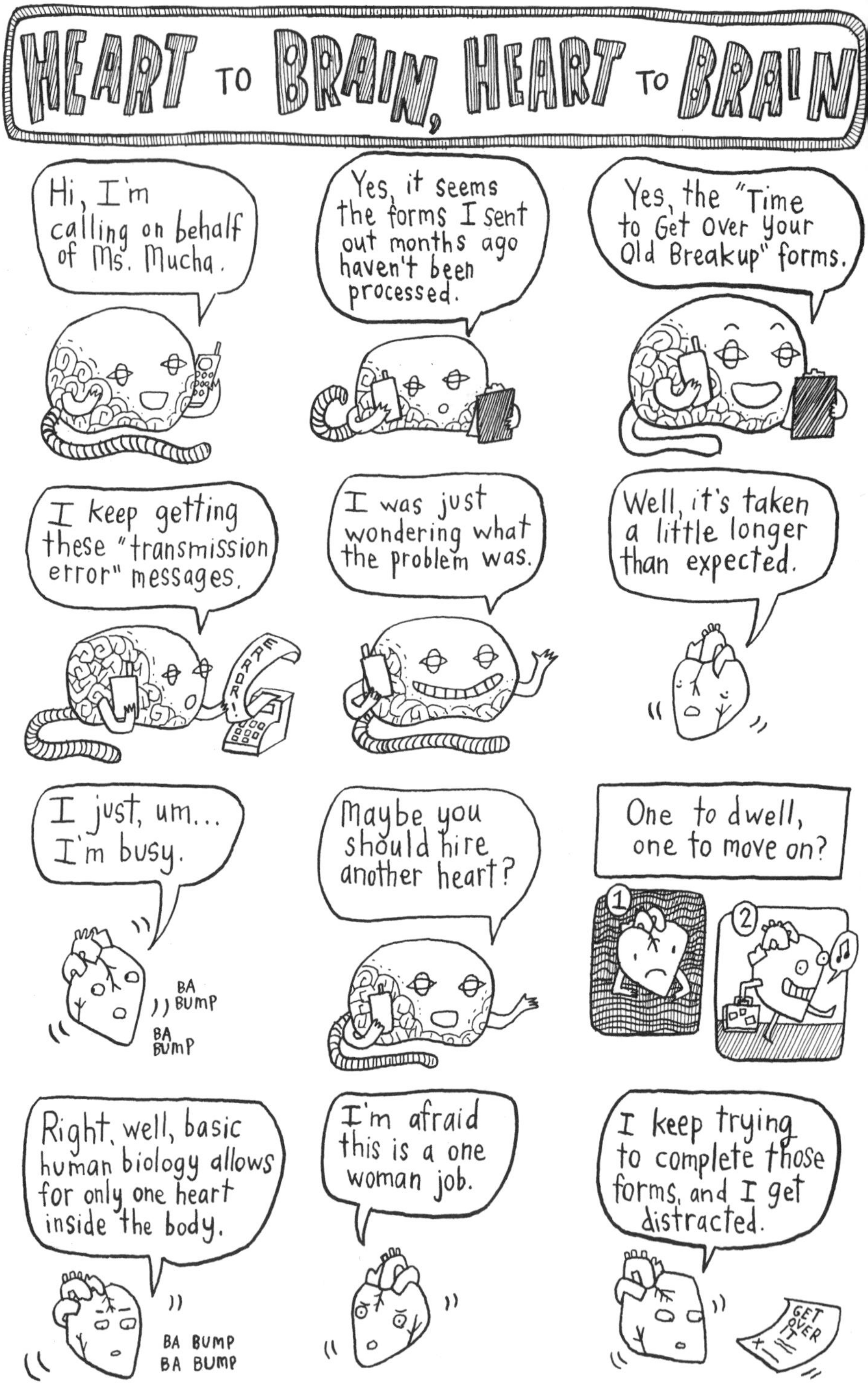
HEART TO BRAIN, HEART TO BRAIN
Hi, I'm calling on behalf of Ms. Mucha.
Yes, it seems the forms I sent out months ago haven't been processed.
Yes, the "Time to Get Over Your Old Breakup" forms.
I keep getting these "transmission error" messages.
ERROR!
I was just wondering what the problem was.
Well, it's taken a little longer than expected.
I just, um... I'm busy.
BA BUMP
BA BUMP
Maybe you should hire another heart?
One to dwell, one to move on?
1
2
Right, well, basic human biology allows for only one heart inside the body.
BA BUMP
BA BUMP
I'm afraid this is a one woman job.
I keep trying to complete those forms, and I get distracted.
GET OVER IT

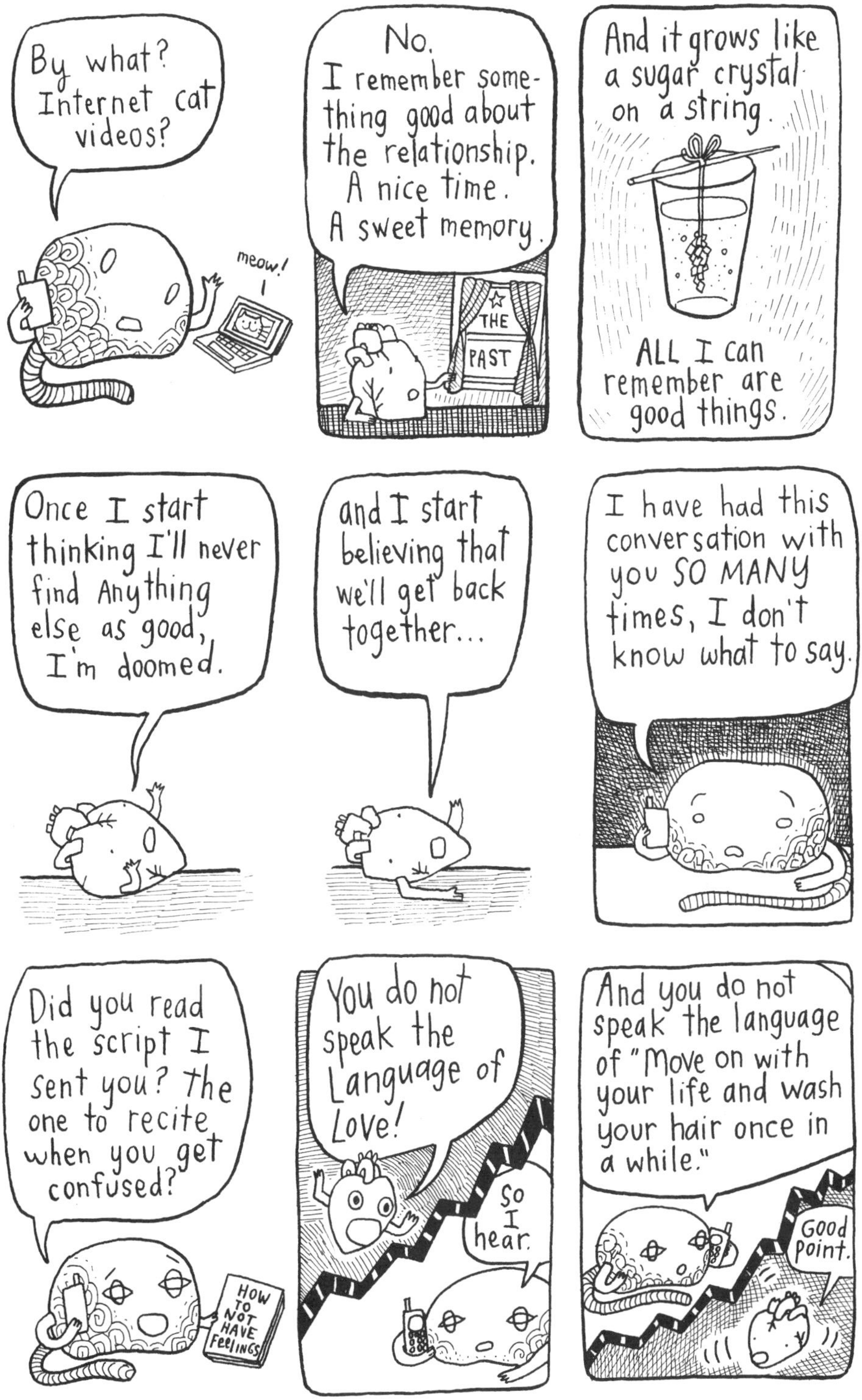
By what? Internet cat videos?
meow!
No. I remember something good about the relationship. A nice time. A sweet memory.
THE PAST
And it grows like a sugar crystal on a string.
ALL I can remember are good things.
Once I start thinking I'll never find Anything else as good, I'm doomed.
and I start believing that we'll get back together...
I have had this conversation with you SO MANY times, I don't know what to say.
Did you read the script I sent you? the one to recite when you get confused?
HOW TO NOT HAVE FEELINGS
You do not speak the Language of Love!
So I hear.
And you do not speak the language of "Move on with your life and wash your hair once in a while."
Good Point.

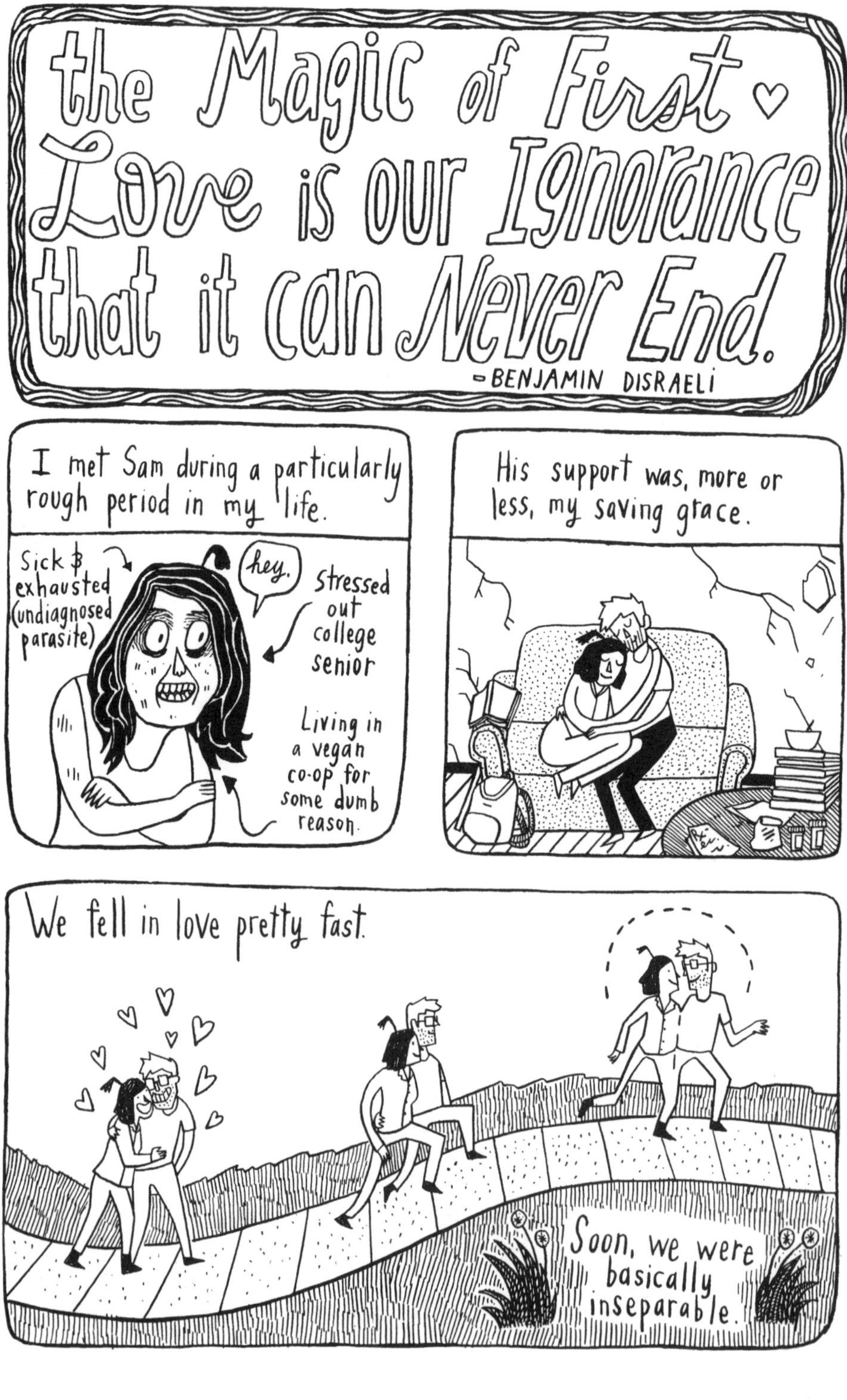

the Magic of First Love is our Ignorance that it can Never End.
-BENJAMIN DISRAELI
I met Sam during a particularly rough period in my life.
Sick & exhausted (undiagnosed parasite)
hey.
Stressed out college senior
Living in a vegan co-op for some dumb reason.
His support was, more or less, my saving grace.
We fell in love pretty fast.
Soon, we were basically inseparable.

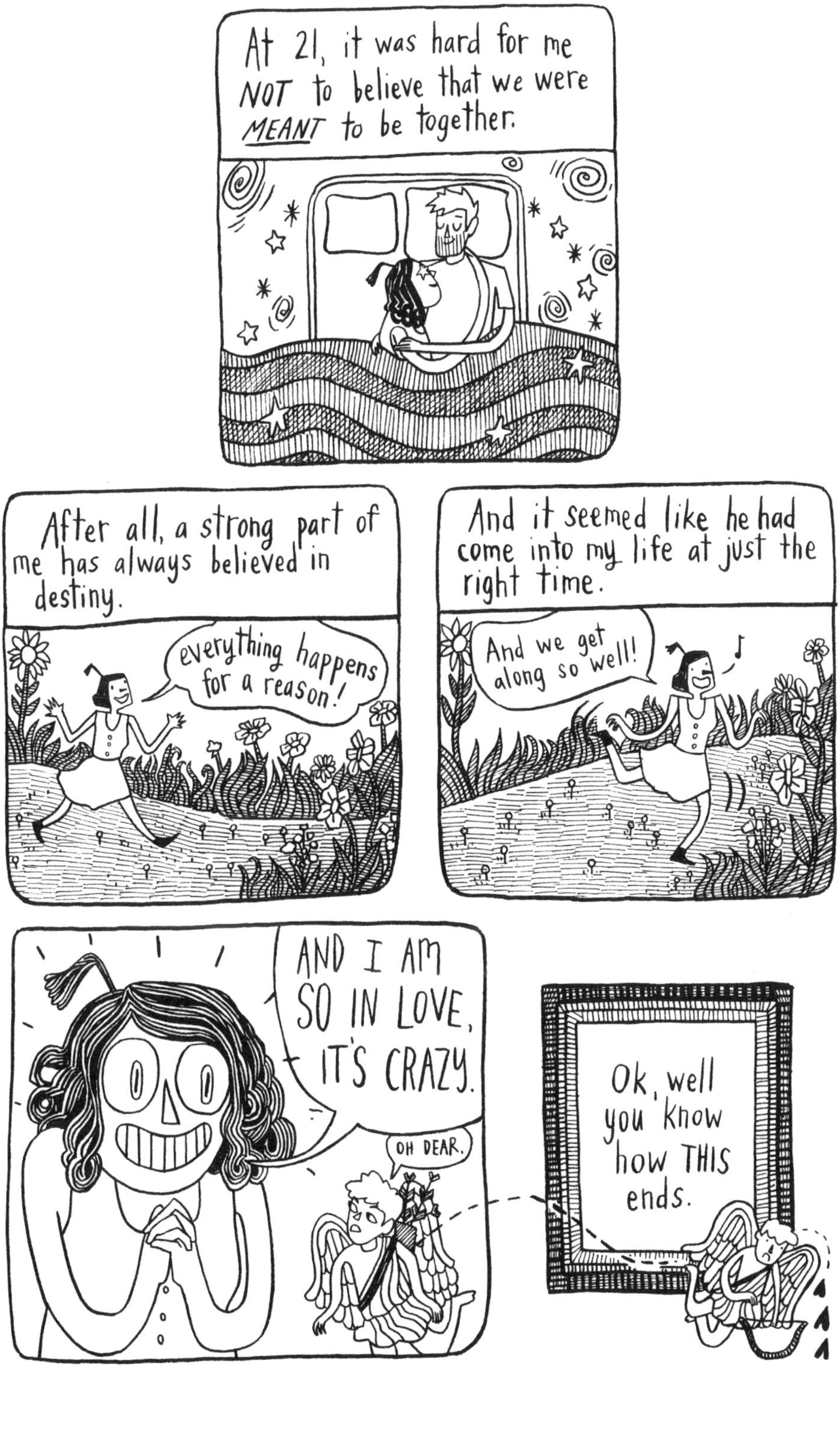
At 21, it was hard for me NOT to believe that we were MEANT to be together.
After all, a strong part of me has always believed in destiny.
everything happens for a reason!
And it seemed like he had come into my life at just the right time.
And we get along so well!
AND I AM SO IN LOVE, IT'S CRAZY.
OH DEAR.
Ok, well you know how THIS ends.

Post breakup, I had a hard time believing there could be other people who were "better" for me.

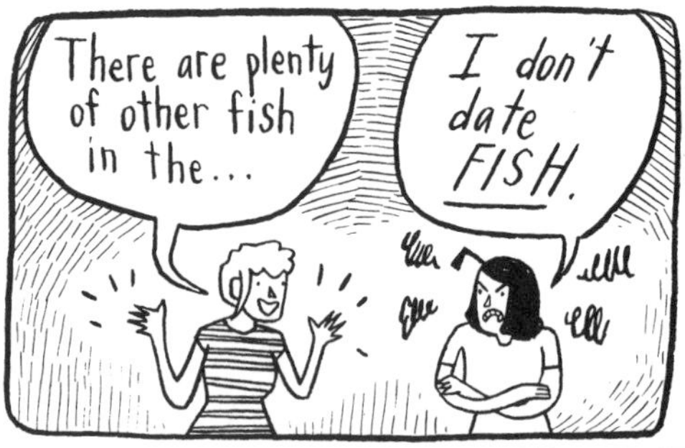
There are plenty of other fish in the...
I don't date FISH.

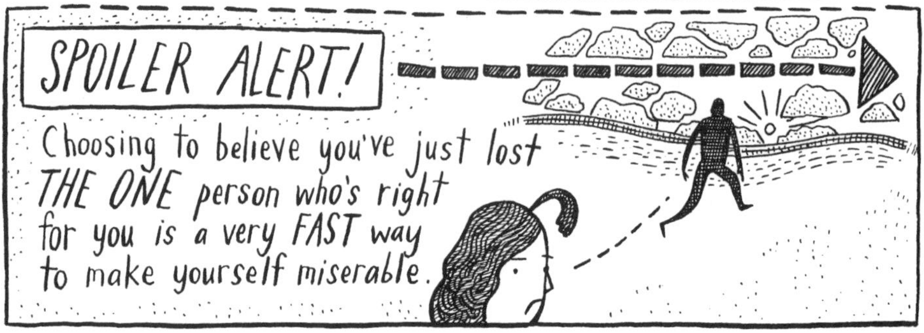
SPOILER ALERT!
Choosing to believe you've just lost THE ONE person who's right for you is a very FAST way to make yourself miserable.

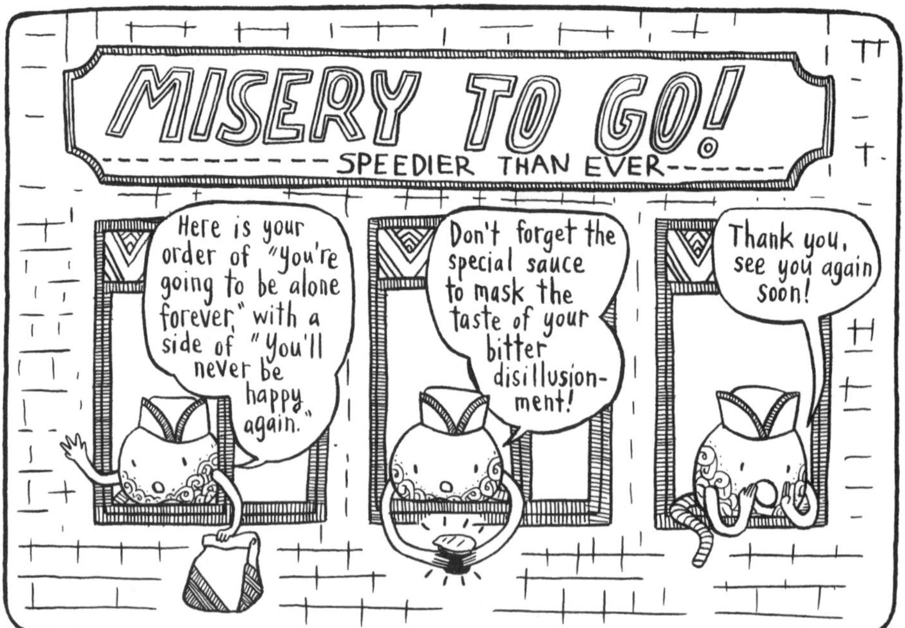
MISERY TO GO!
SPEEDIER THAN EVER
Here is your order of "You're going to be alone forever," with a side of "You'll never be happy again."
Don't forget the special sauce to mask the taste of your bitter disillusionment!
Thank you, see you again soon!

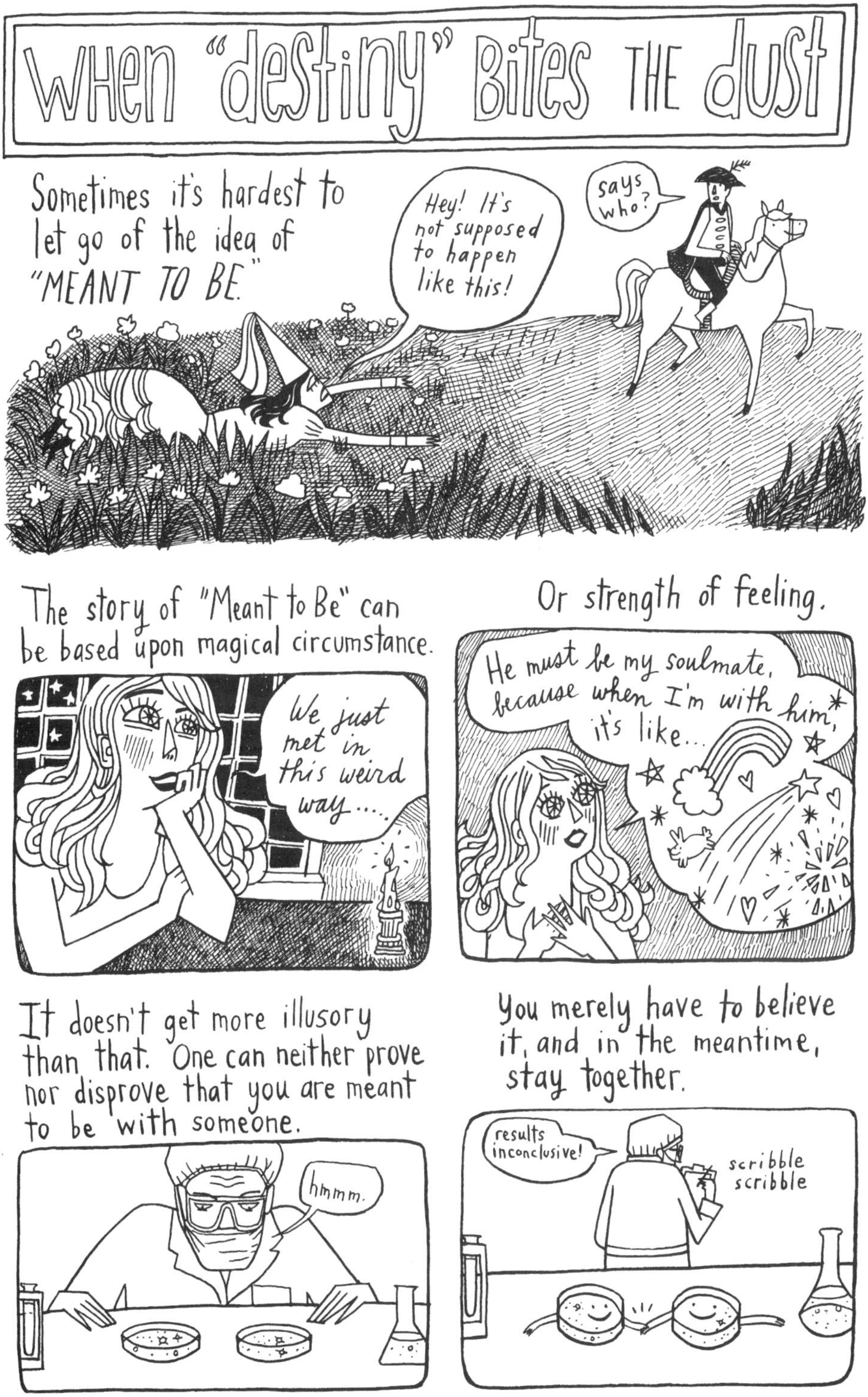
WHEN "DESTINY" BITES THE DUST
Sometimes it's hardest to let go of the idea of "MEANT TO BE."
Hey! It's not supposed to happen like this!
says who?
The story of "Meant to Be" can be based upon magical circumstance.
We just met in this weird way....
Or strength of feeling.
He must be my soulmate, because when I'm with him, it's like...
It doesn't get more illusory than that. One can neither prove nor disprove that you are meant to be with someone.
hmmm.
You merely have to believe it, and in the meantime, stay together.
results inconclusive!
scribble scribble

SO, what happens, then, when you break up, but you still believe you are meant to be together?

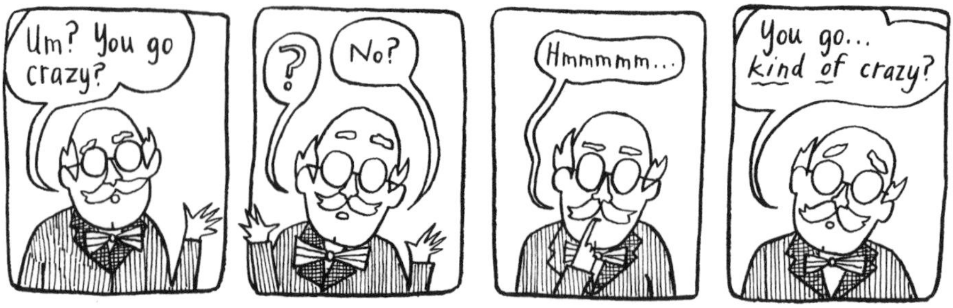
Um? You go crazy?
?
No?
Hmmmmm...
You go... kind of crazy?

In the movies, this is where one lover does not give up.

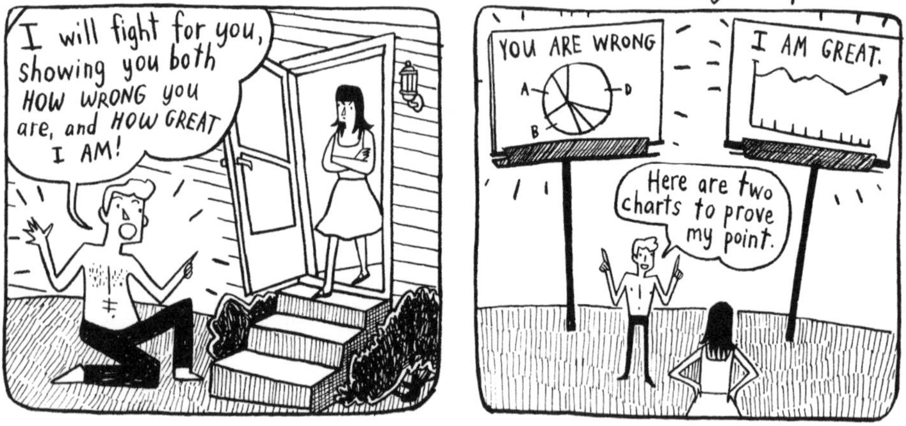
I will fight for you, showing you both HOW WRONG you are, and HOW GREAT I AM!
YOU ARE WRONG
A
B
D
I AM GREAT.
Here are two charts to prove my point.

The happy ending is when they are together again.

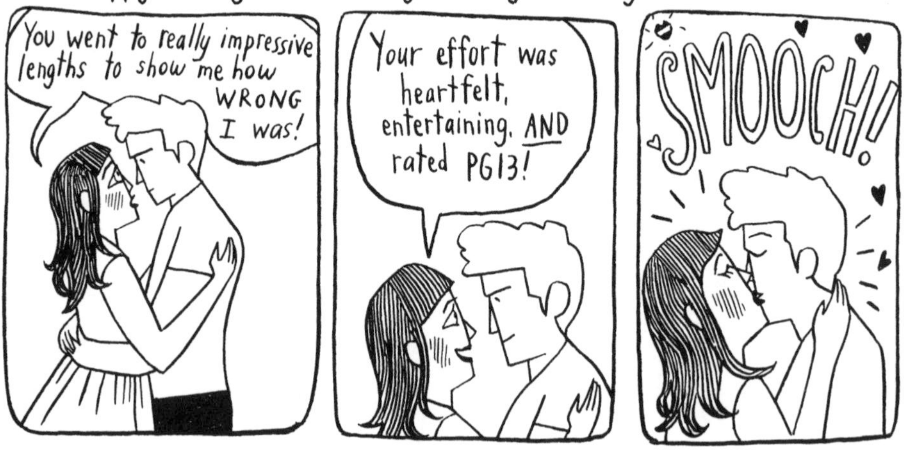
You went to really impressive lengths to show me how WRONG I was!
Your effort was heartfelt, entertaining, AND rated PG13!
SMOOCH!

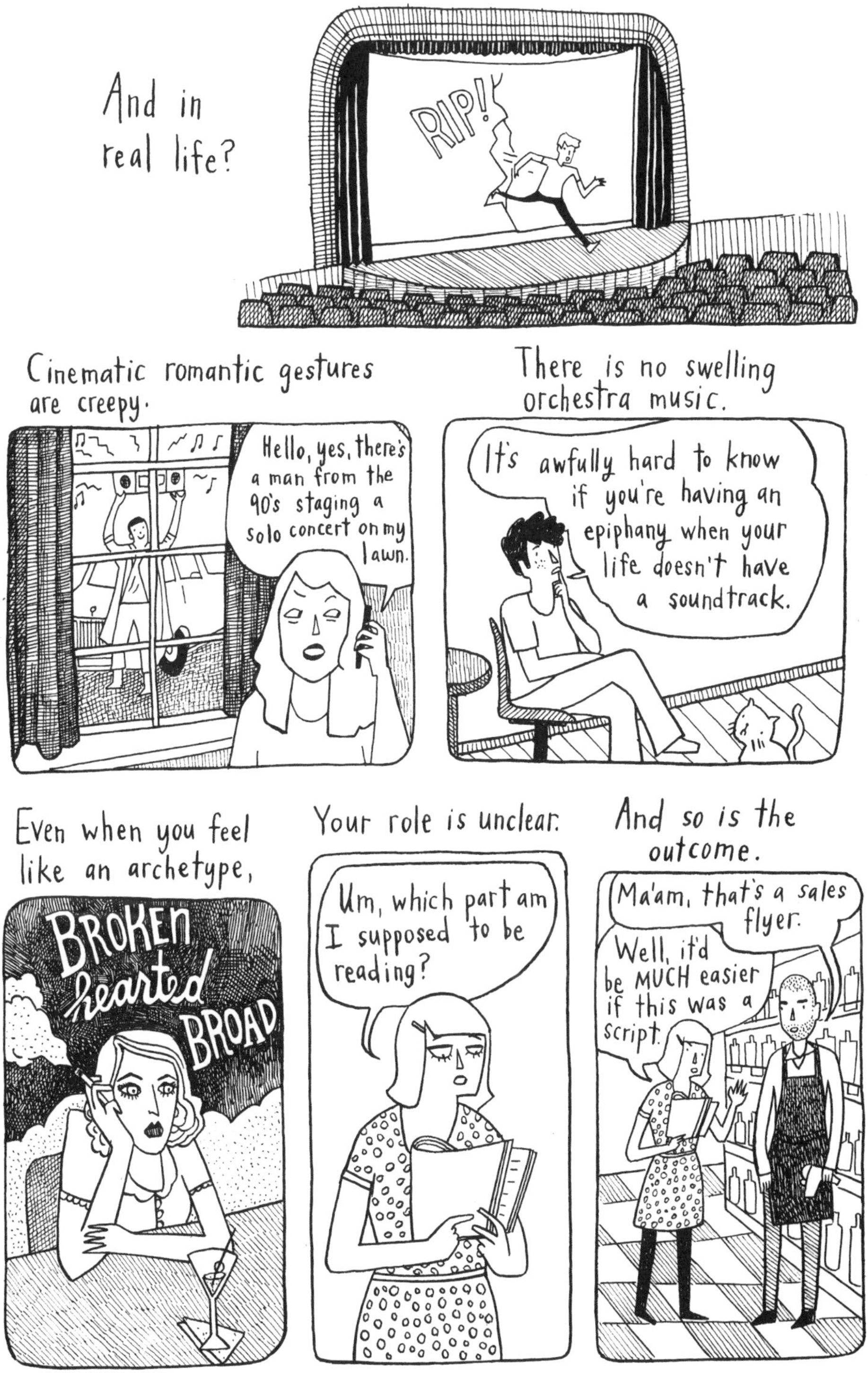
And in real life?
RIP!
Cinematic romantic gestures are creepy.
Hello, yes, there's a man from the 90's staging a solo concert on my lawn.
There is no swelling orchestra music.
It's awfully hard to know if you're having an epiphany when your life doesn't have a soundtrack.
Even when you feel like an archetype,
BROKEN hearted BROAD
Your role is unclear.
Um, which part am I supposed to be reading?
And so is the outcome.
Ma'am, that's a sales flyer.
Well, it'd be MUCH easier if this was a script.

The Relationship in Your Head

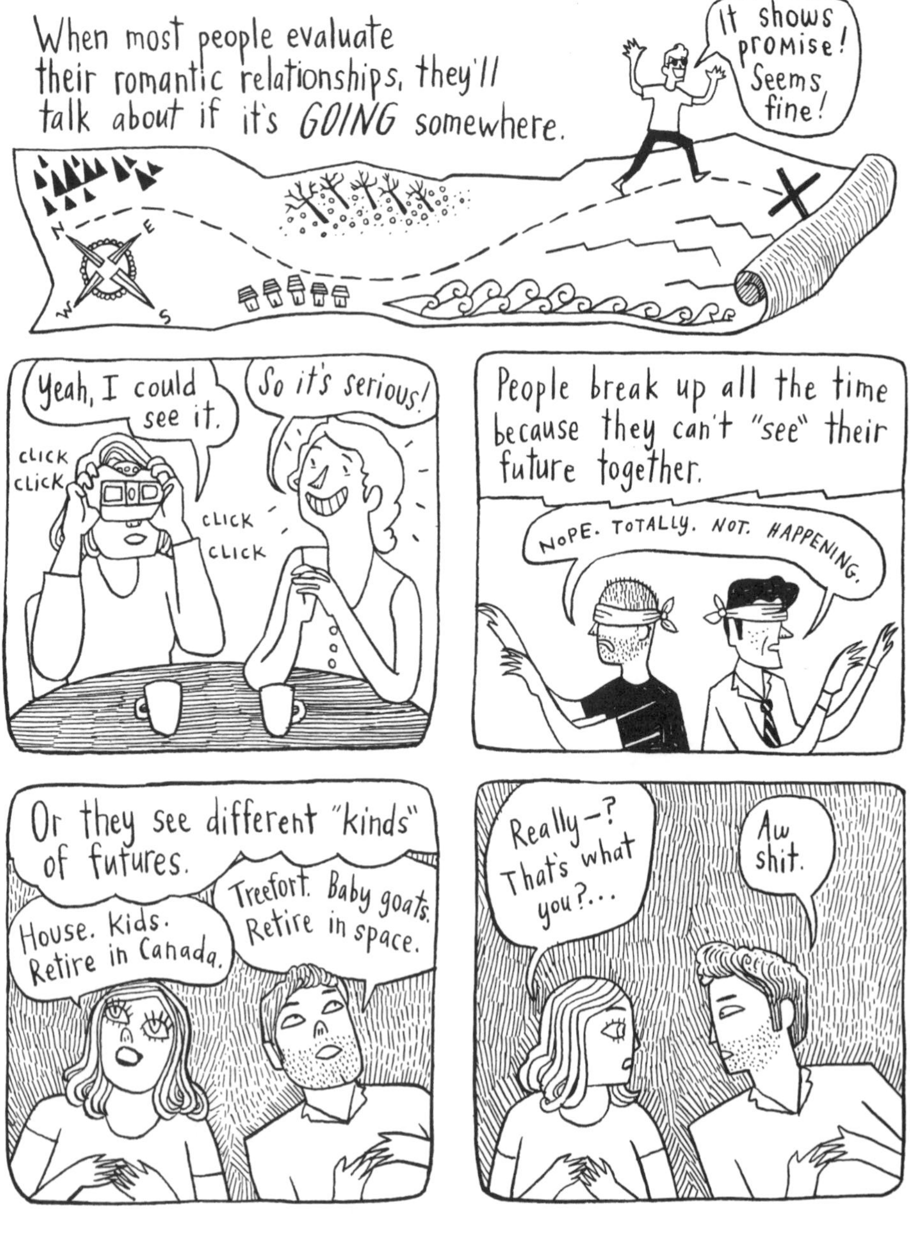

When most people evaluate their romantic relationships, they'll talk about if it's *GOING* somewhere.
It shows promise! Seems fine!
N
E
W
S
Yeah, I could see it.
So it's serious!
CLICK CLICK
CLICK CLICK
People break up all the time because they can't "see" their future together.
NOPE. TOTALLY. NOT. HAPPENING.
Or they see different "kinds" of futures.
House. Kids. Retire in Canada.
Treefort. Baby goats. Retire in space.
Really–? That's what you?...
Aw shit.

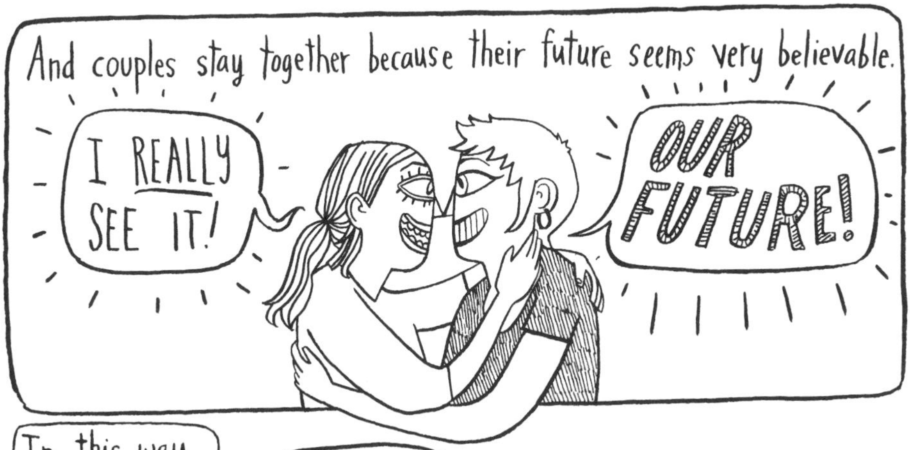
And couples stay together because their future seems very believable.
I REALLY SEE IT!
OUR FUTURE!

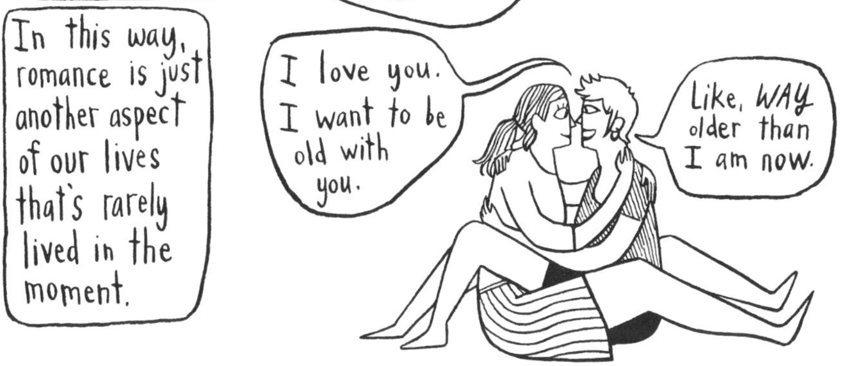
In this way, romance is just another aspect of our lives that's rarely lived in the moment.
I love you. I want to be old with you.
Like, WAY older than I am now.

It's truly maddening.

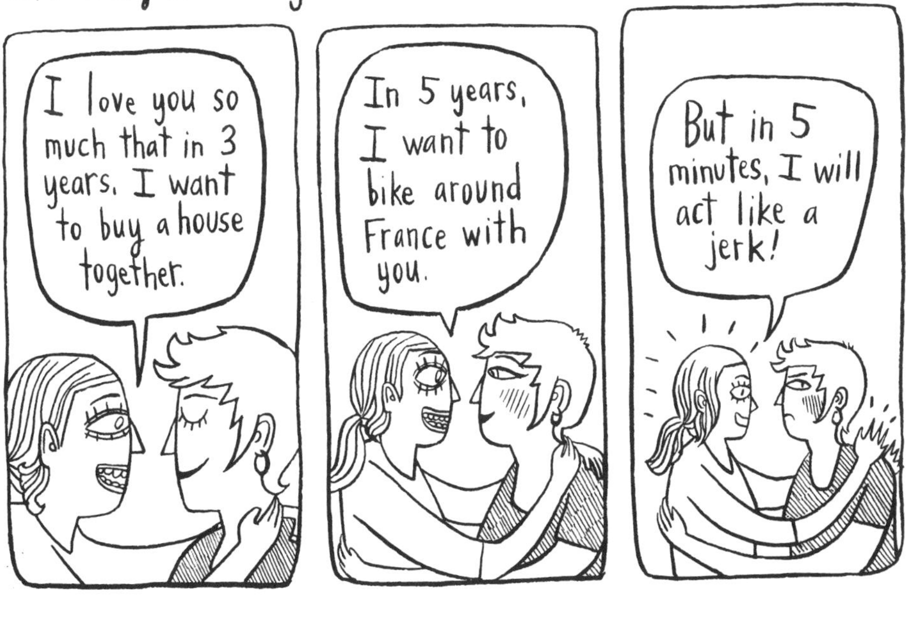
I love you so much that in 3 years, I want to buy a house together.
In 5 years, I want to bike around France with you.
But in 5 minutes, I will act like a jerk!

During a breakup, there is the real life to let go of.

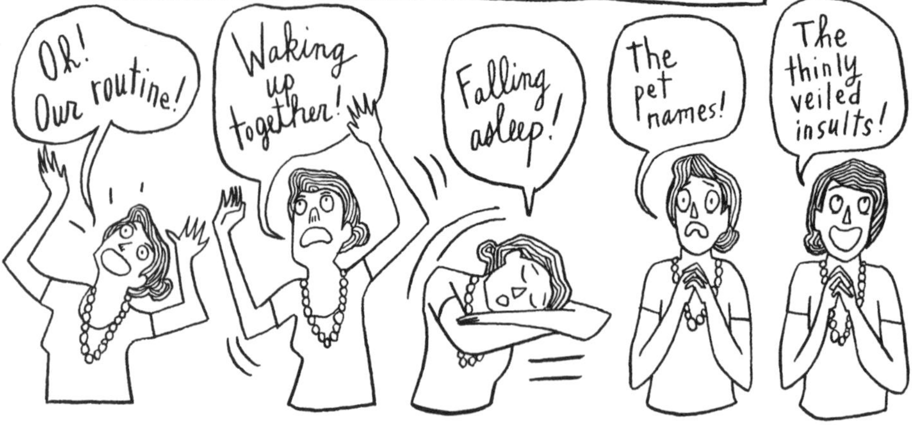
Oh! Our routine!
Waking up together!
Falling asleep!
The pet names!
The thinly veiled insults!

BUT there is also the IMAGINED one.

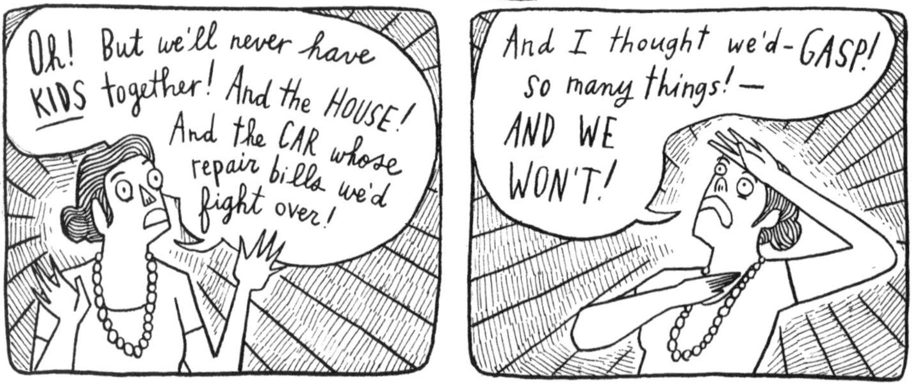
Oh! But we'll never have KIDS together! And the HOUSE! And the CAR whose repair bills we'd fight over!
And I thought we'd - GASP! so many things! — AND WE WON'T!

As a person who spends a lot of time dwelling in their imagination, this was particularly hard for me.

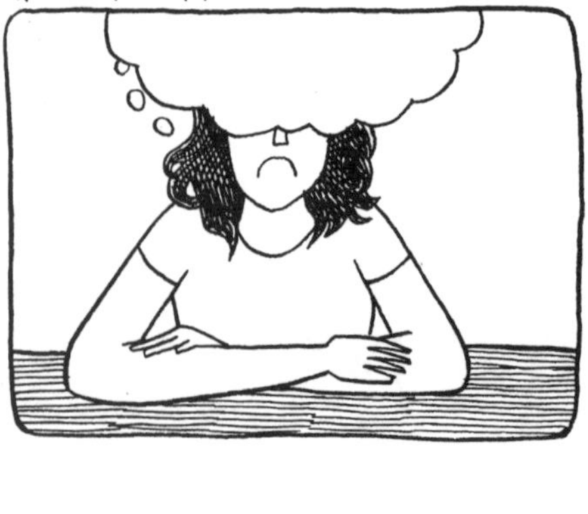

I'd spun stories that felt SO believable.

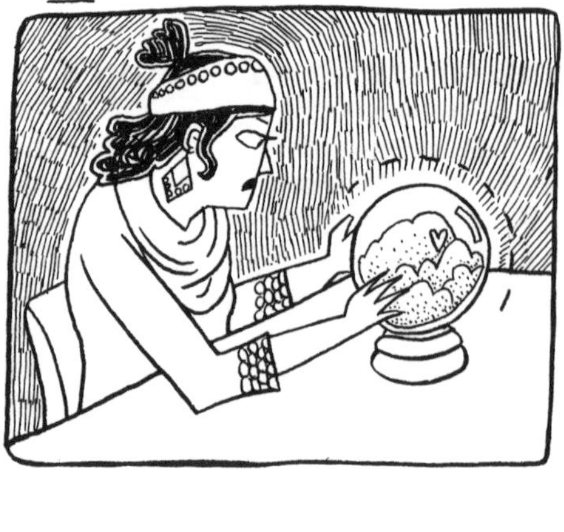

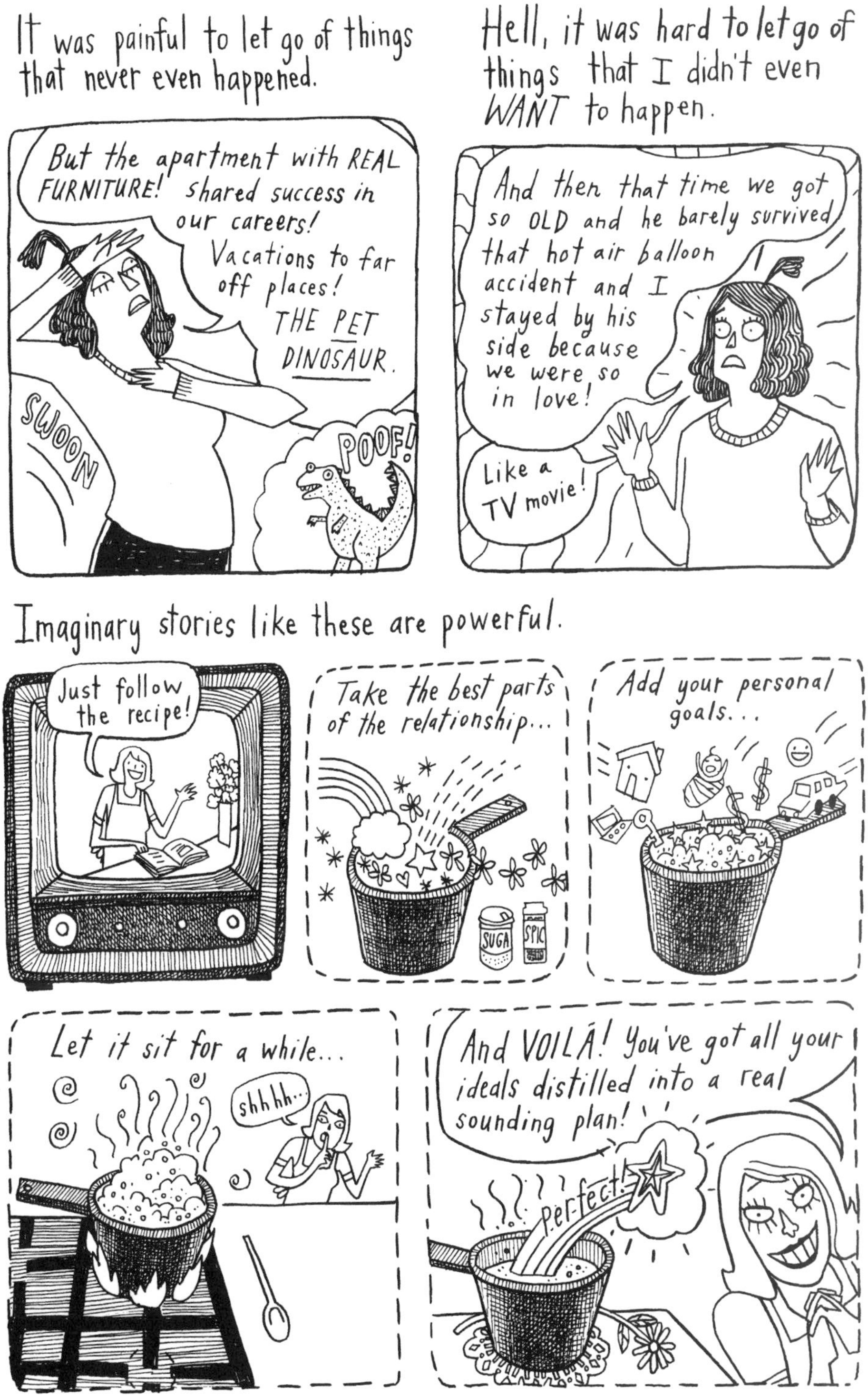
It was painful to let go of things that never even happened.
Hell, it was hard to let go of things that I didn't even WANT to happen.
But the apartment with REAL FURNITURE! Shared success in our careers! Vacations to far off places! THE PET DINOSAUR.
SWOON
POOF!
And then that time we got so OLD and he barely survived that hot air balloon accident and I stayed by his side because we were so in love!
Like a TV movie!
Imaginary stories like these are powerful.
Just follow the recipe!
Take the best parts of the relationship...
SUGA
SPIC
Add your personal goals...
Let it sit for a while...
shhhh...
And VOILÀ! You've got all your ideals distilled into a real sounding plan!
perfect!

A breakup can feel like an unjust beheading of your dreams.

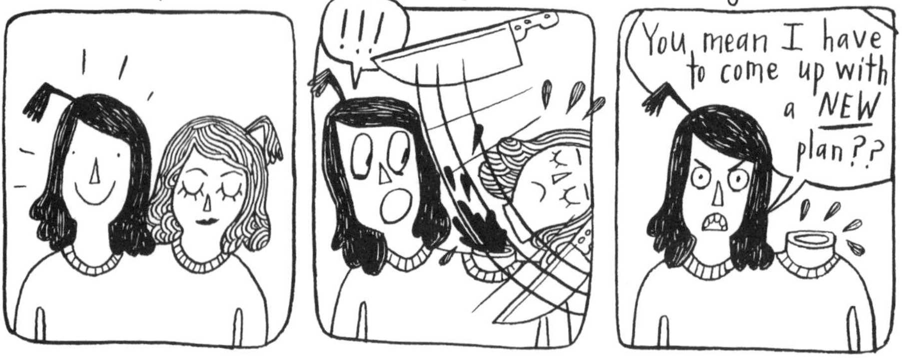
!!!
You mean I have to come up with a NEW plan??

Maybe one of the hardest parts of accepting change is acknowledging the death of that phantom limb—your unlived plans.

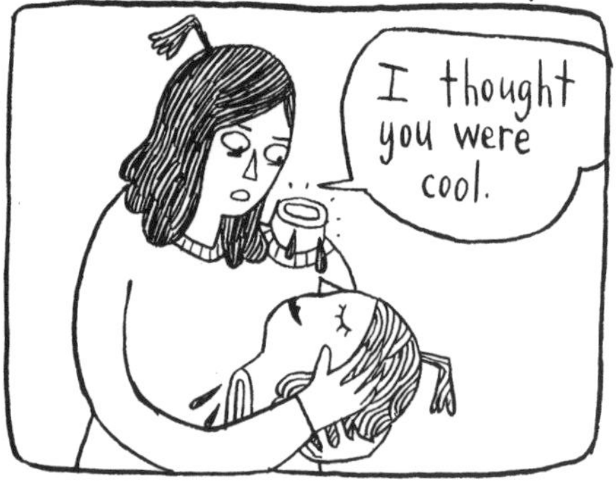
I thought you were cool.

Because at the center of this is also the person you thought you might be.

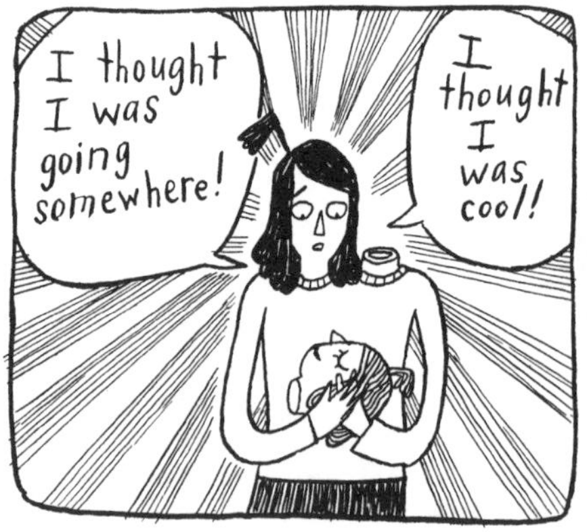
I thought I was going somewhere!
I thought I was cool!

And what's a bigger buzzkill than being reminded that you're not unique—you're just as vulnerable to change and uncertainty as every other living sucker.

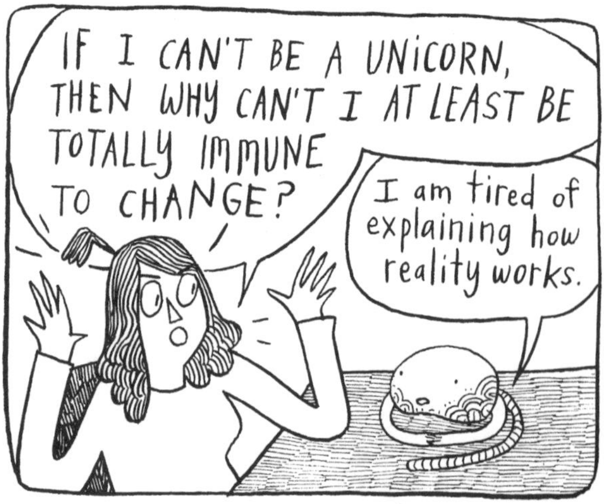
IF I CAN'T BE A UNICORN, THEN WHY CAN'T I AT LEAST BE TOTALLY IMMUNE TO CHANGE?
I am tired of explaining how reality works.

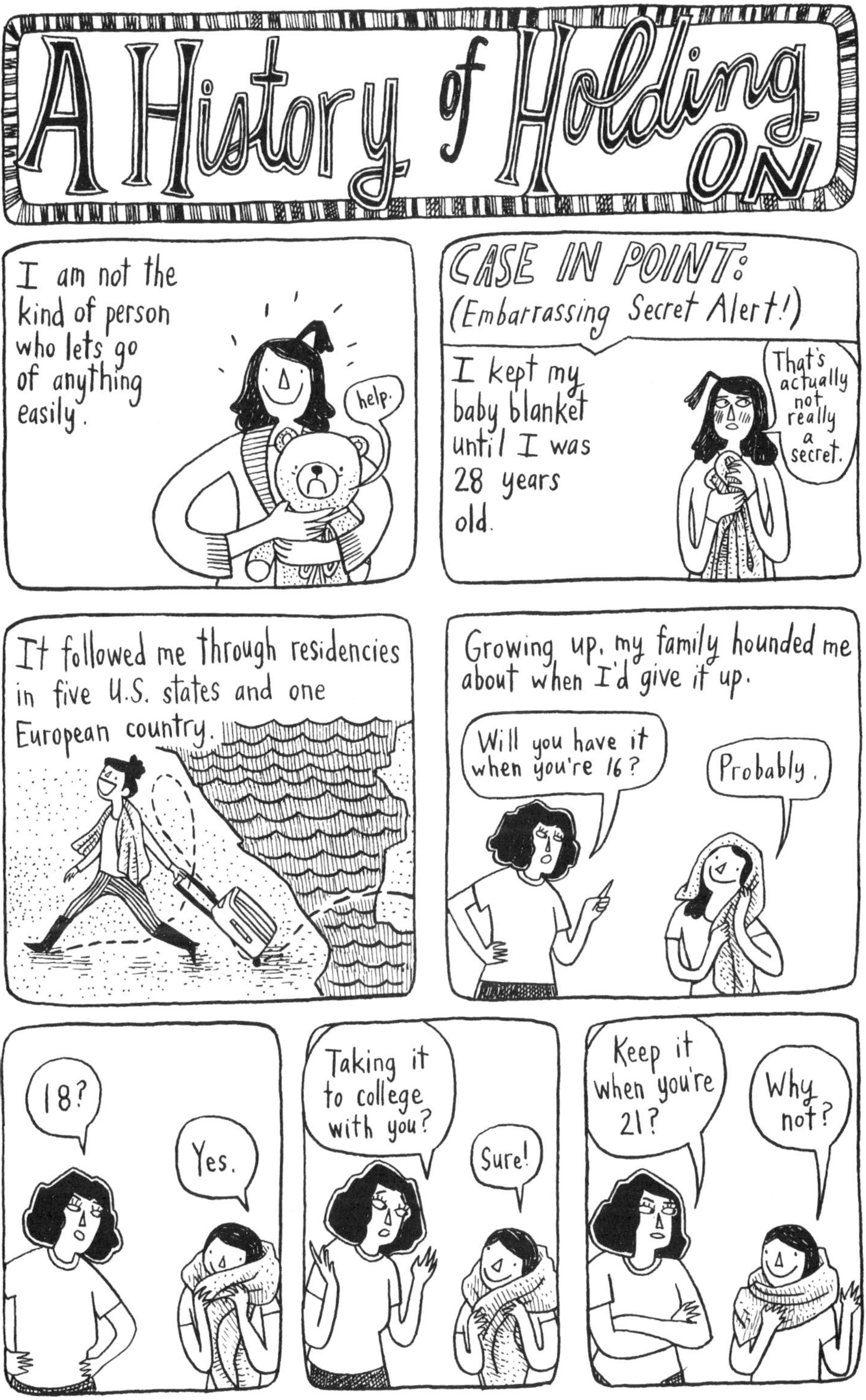
A History of Holding ON
I am not the kind of person who lets go of anything easily.
help.
CASE IN POINT:
(Embarrassing Secret Alert!)
I kept my baby blanket until I was 28 years old.
That's actually not really a secret.
It followed me through residencies in five U.S. states and one European country.
Growing up, my family hounded me about when I'd give it up.
Will you have it when you're 16?
Probably.
18?
Yes.
Taking it to college with you?
Sure!
Keep it when you're 21?
Why not?

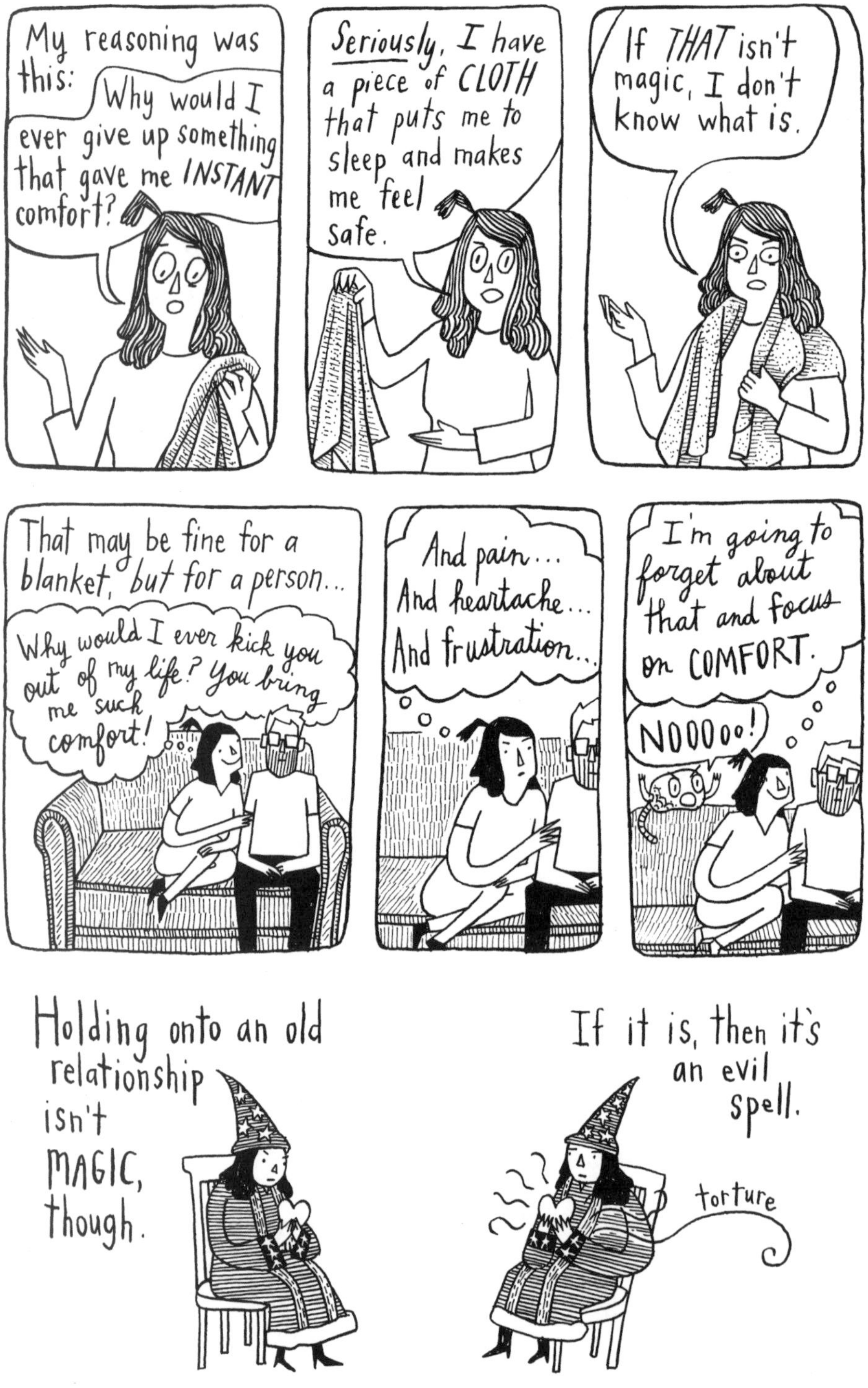
My reasoning was this:
Why would I ever give up something that gave me INSTANT comfort?
Seriously, I have a piece of CLOTH that puts me to sleep and makes me feel safe.
If THAT isn't magic, I don't know what is.
That may be fine for a blanket, but for a person...
Why would I ever kick you out of my life? You bring me such comfort!
And pain...
And heartache...
And frustration...
I'm going to forget about that and focus on COMFORT.
NOOOoo!
Holding onto an old relationship isn't MAGIC, though.
If it is, then it's an evil spell.
torture

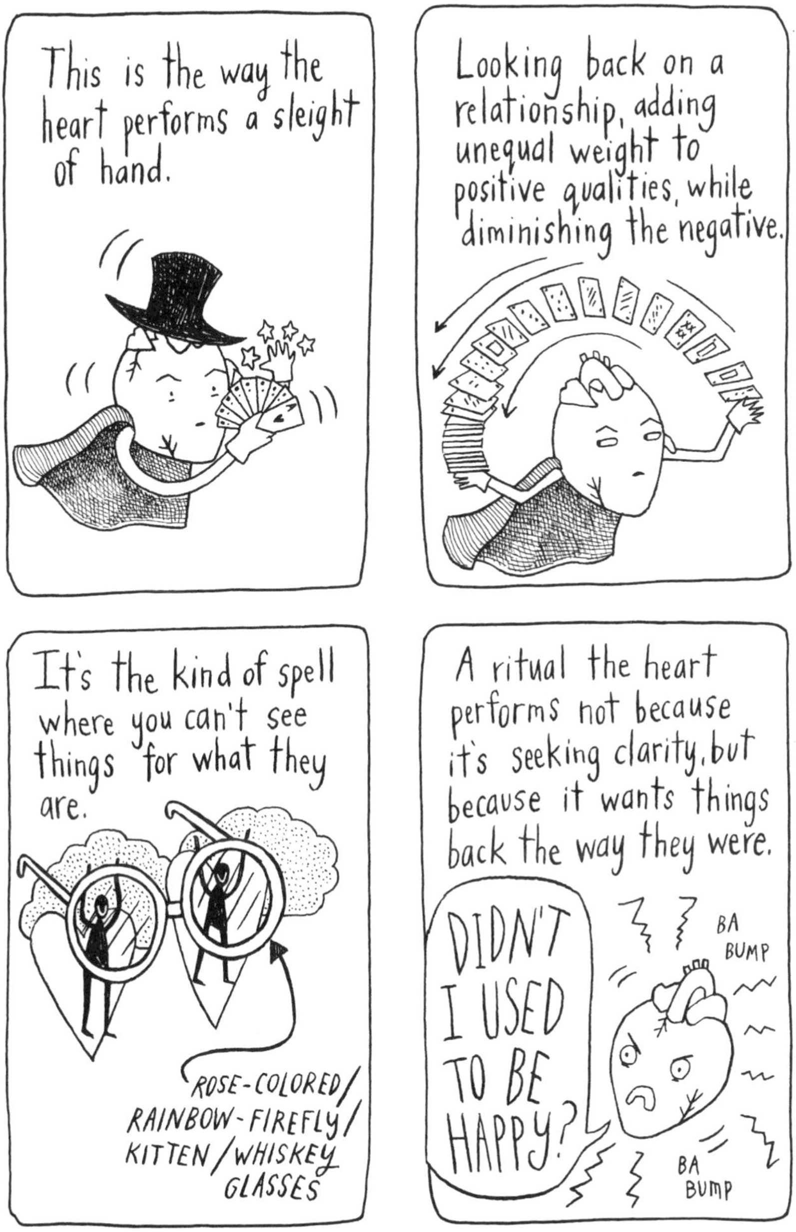

This is the way the heart performs a sleight of hand.
Looking back on a relationship, adding unequal weight to positive qualities, while diminishing the negative.
It's the kind of spell where you can't see things for what they are.
ROSE-COLORED/RAINBOW-FIREFLY/KITTEN/WHISKEY GLASSES
A ritual the heart performs not because it's seeking clarity, but because it wants things back the way they were.
DIDN'T I USED TO BE HAPPY?
BA BUMP
BA BUMP

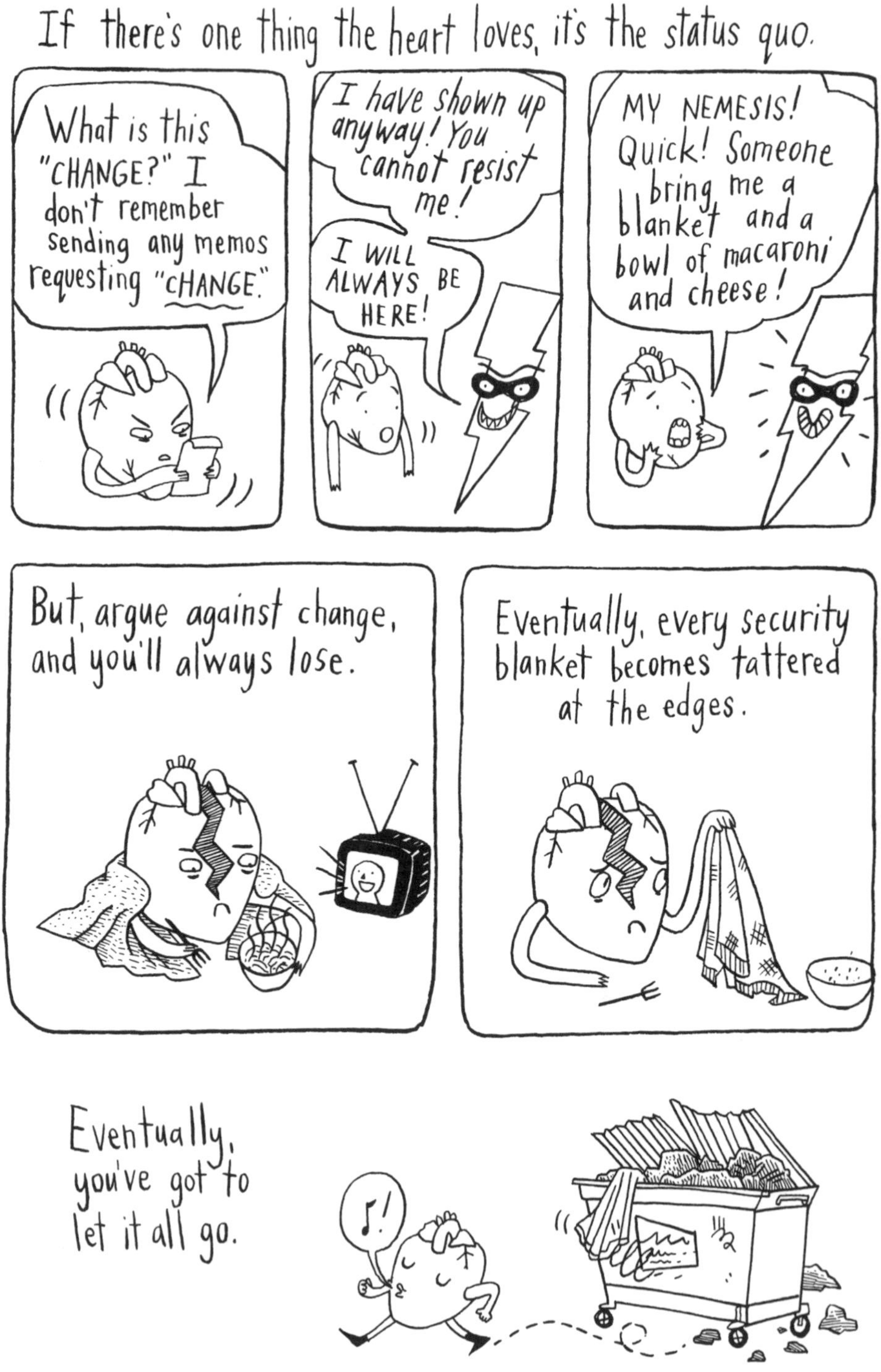
If there's one thing the heart loves, it's the status quo.
What is this "CHANGE?" I don't remember sending any memos requesting "CHANGE."
I have shown up anyway! You cannot resist me!
I WILL ALWAYS BE HERE!
MY NEMESIS! Quick! Someone bring me a blanket and a bowl of macaroni and cheese!
But, argue against change, and you'll always lose.
Eventually, every security blanket becomes tattered at the edges.
Eventually, you've got to let it all go.

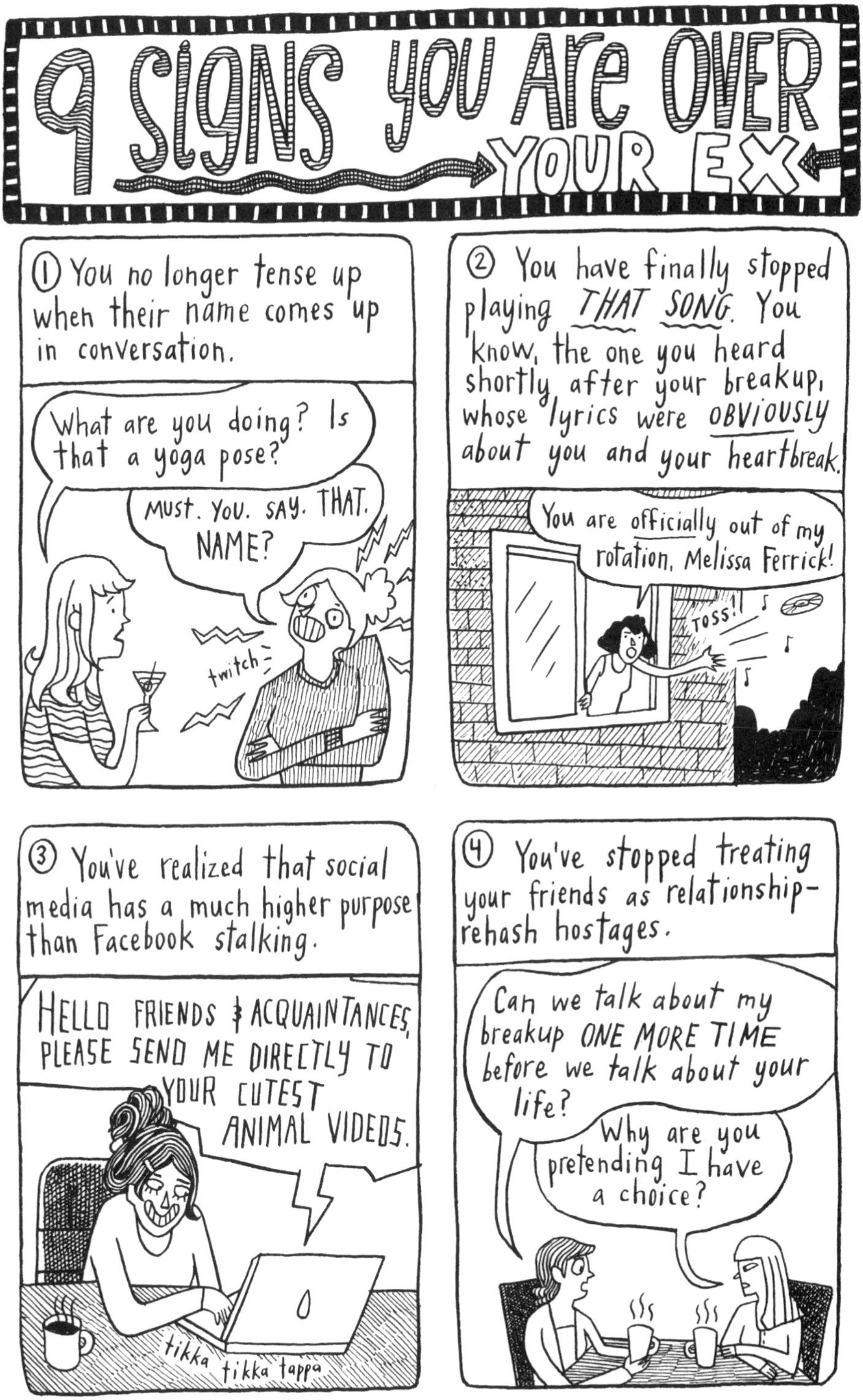
9 SIGNS YOU ARE OVER YOUR EX
① You no longer tense up when their name comes up in conversation.
What are you doing? Is that a yoga pose?
MUST. YOU. SAY. THAT. NAME?
twitch
② You have finally stopped playing THAT SONG. You know, the one you heard shortly after your breakup, whose lyrics were OBVIOUSLY about you and your heartbreak.
You are officially out of my rotation, Melissa Ferrick!
TOSS!
③ You've realized that social media has a much higher purpose than Facebook stalking.
HELLO FRIENDS & ACQUAINTANCES, PLEASE SEND ME DIRECTLY TO YOUR CUTEST ANIMAL VIDEOS.
tikka tikka tappa
④ You've stopped treating your friends as relationship-rehash hostages.
Can we talk about my breakup ONE MORE TIME before we talk about your life?
Why are you pretending I have a choice?

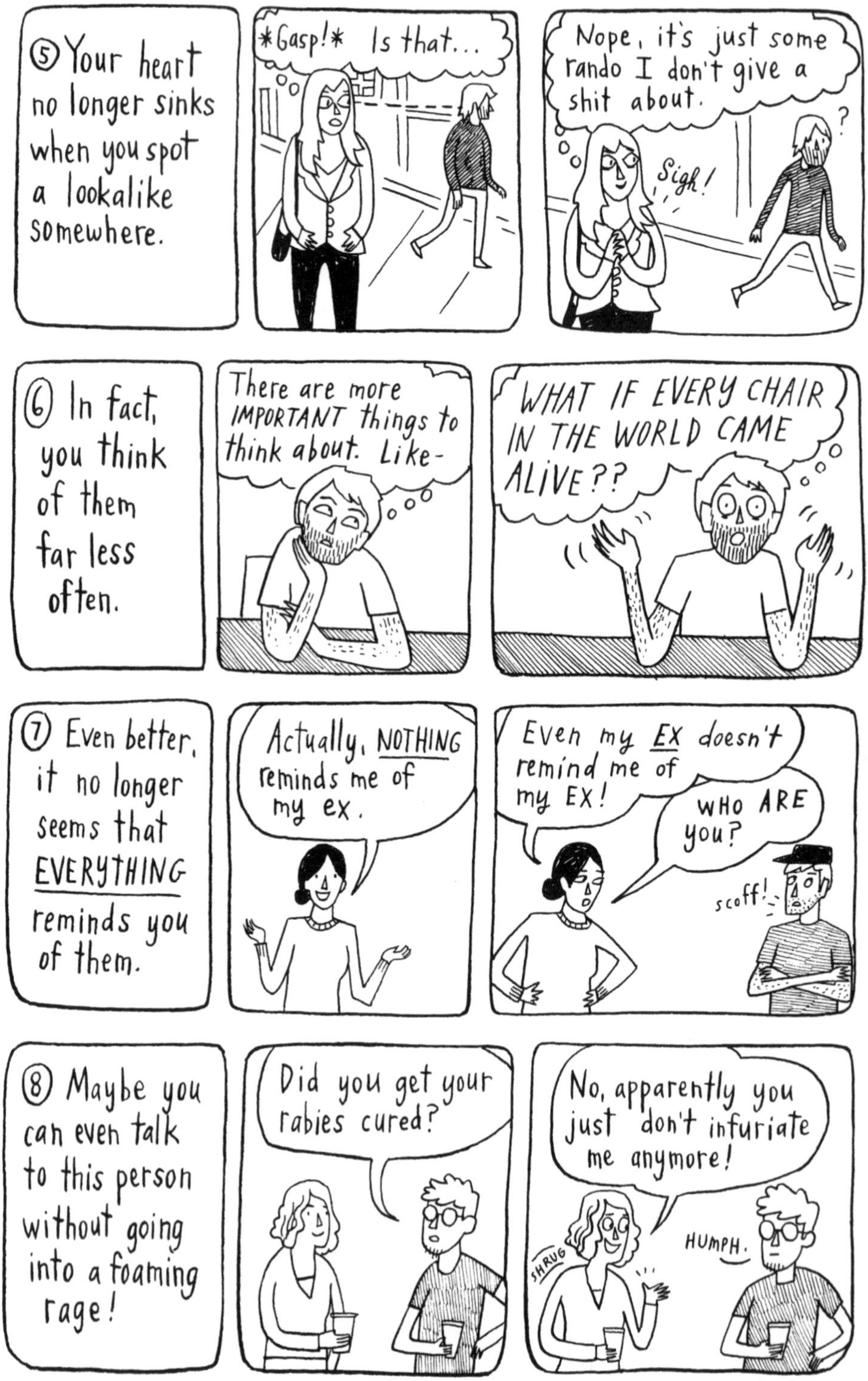
⑤ Your heart no longer sinks when you spot a lookalike somewhere.
Gasp! Is that...
Nope, it's just some rando I don't give a shit about.
Sigh!
?
⑥ In fact, you think of them far less often.
There are more IMPORTANT things to think about. Like-
WHAT IF EVERY CHAIR IN THE WORLD CAME ALIVE??
⑦ Even better, it no longer seems that EVERYTHING reminds you of them.
Actually, NOTHING reminds me of my ex.
Even my EX doesn't remind me of my EX!
WHO ARE you?
scoff!
⑧ Maybe you can even talk to this person without going into a foaming rage!
Did you get your rabies cured?
No, apparently you just don't infuriate me anymore!
SHRUG
HUMPH.

⑨ Most importantly, you no longer see your life as lacking without them in it.

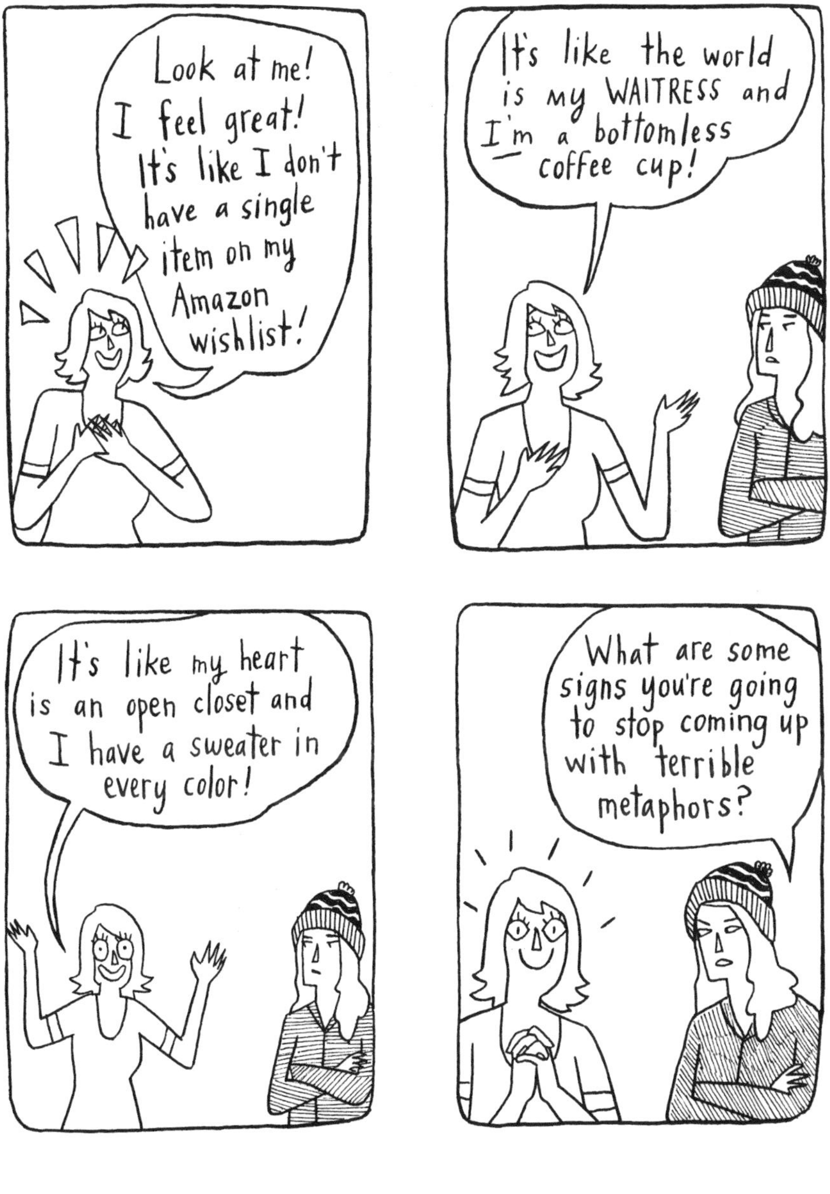
Look at me! I feel great! It's like I don't have a single item on my Amazon wishlist!
It's like the world is my WAITRESS and I'm a bottomless coffee cup!
It's like my heart is an open closet and I have a sweater in every color!
What are some signs you're going to stop coming up with terrible metaphors?

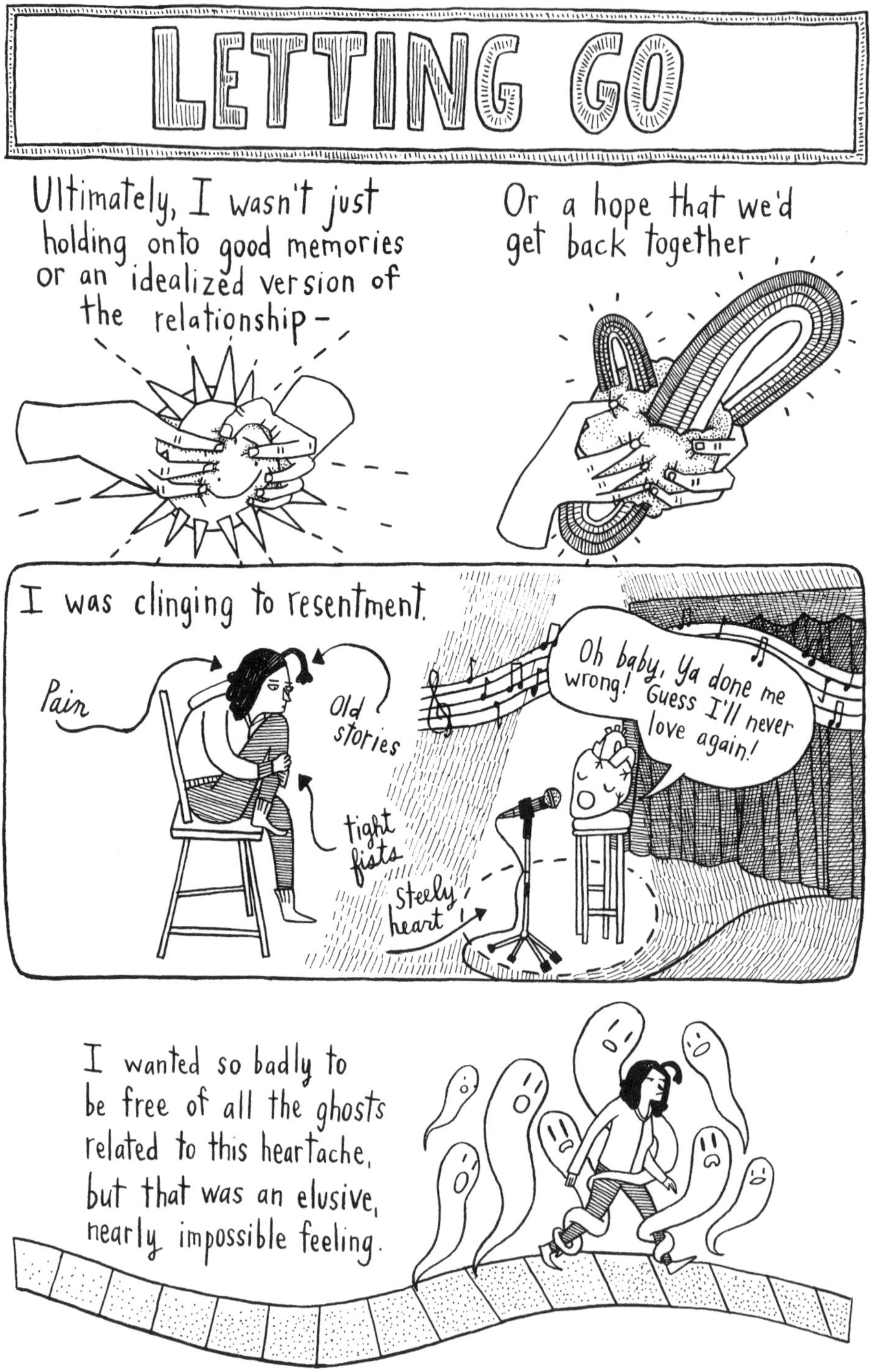
LETTING GO
Ultimately, I wasn't just holding onto good memories or an idealized version of the relationship–
Or a hope that we'd get back together
I was clinging to resentment.
Pain
Old stories
tight fists
Steely heart
Oh baby, Ya done me wrong! Guess I'll never love again!
I wanted so badly to be free of all the ghosts related to this heartache, but that was an elusive, nearly impossible feeling.

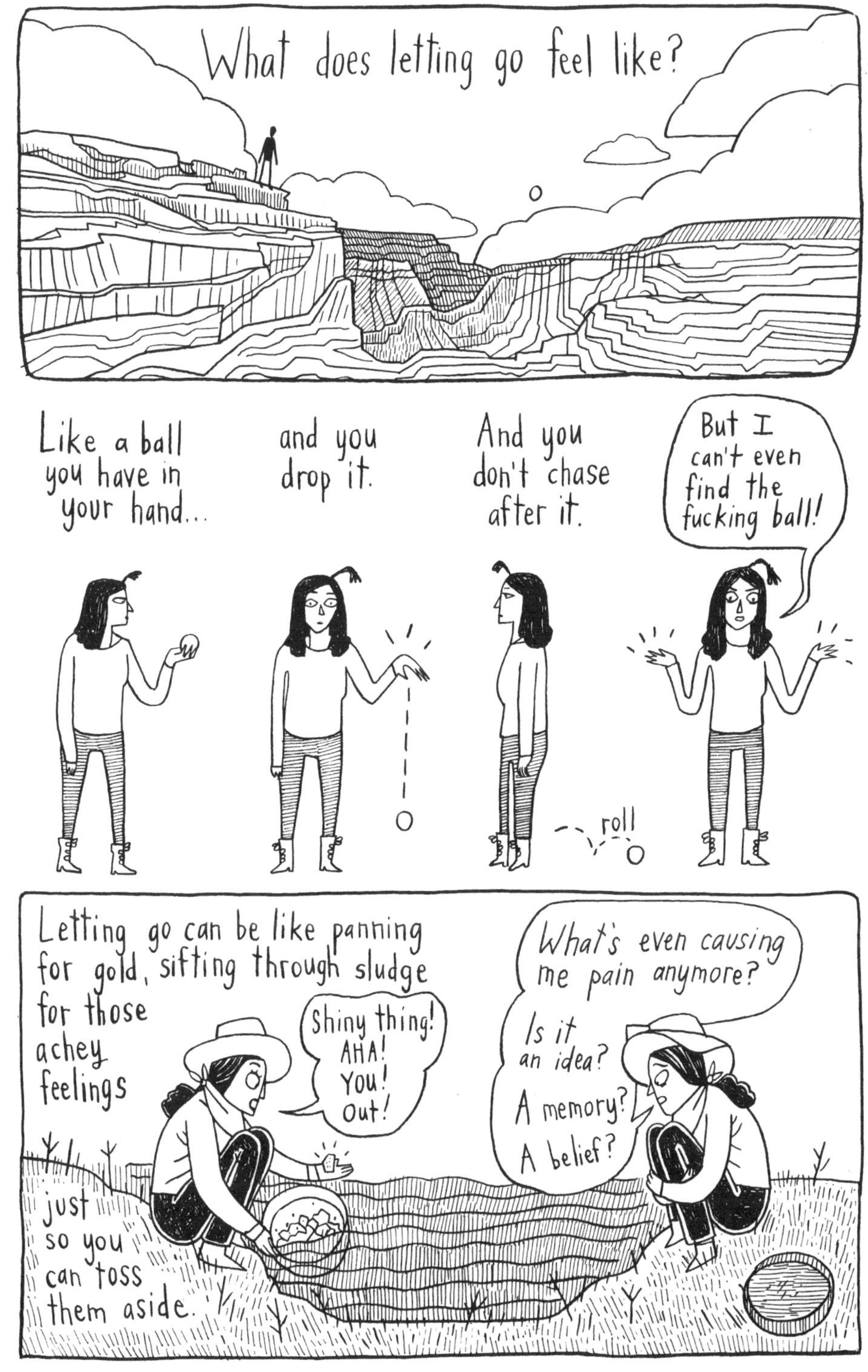
What does letting go feel like?
Like a ball you have in your hand...
and you drop it.
And you don't chase after it.
roll
But I can't even find the fucking ball!
Letting go can be like panning for gold, sifting through sludge for those achey feelings
Shiny thing! AHA! You! Out!
just so you can toss them aside.
What's even causing me pain anymore?
Is it an idea?
A memory?
A belief?

I wished I could invent a magnet to swallow, that would attract everything I no longer needed.

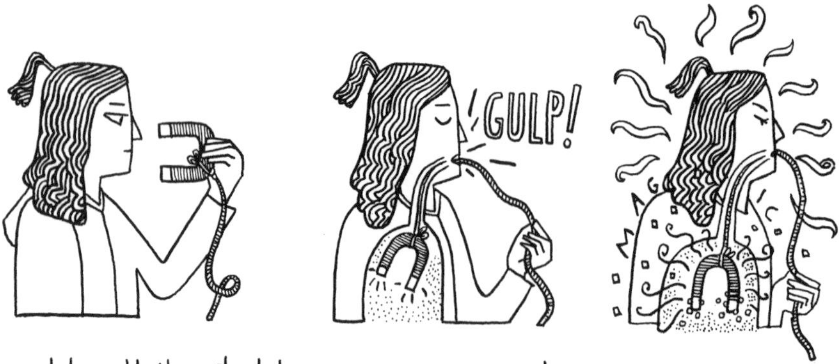
GULP!
MAGIC

I could pull it out, like a con man's quarter in a vending machine.

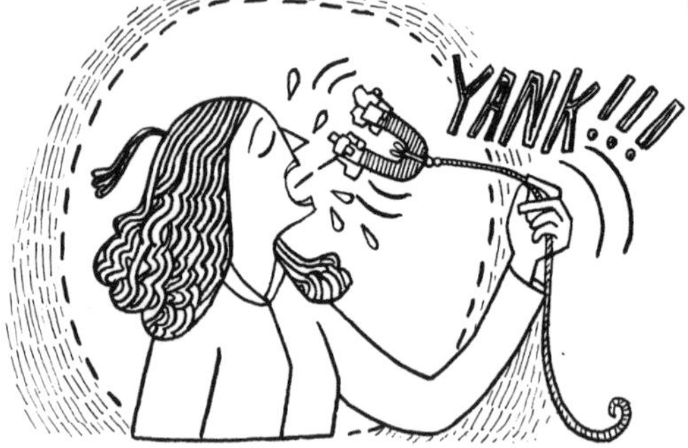
YANK!!!!

Then drop it in a *HOLY RIVER*, or a bowl of *ACID*.

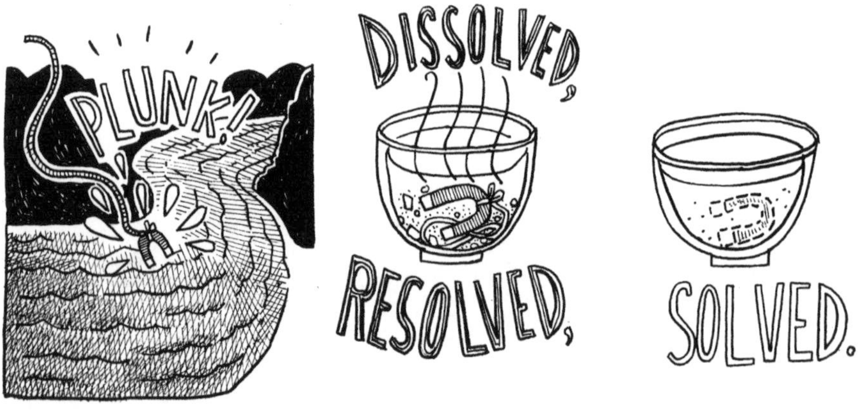
PLUNK!
DISSOLVED,
RESOLVED,
SOLVED.

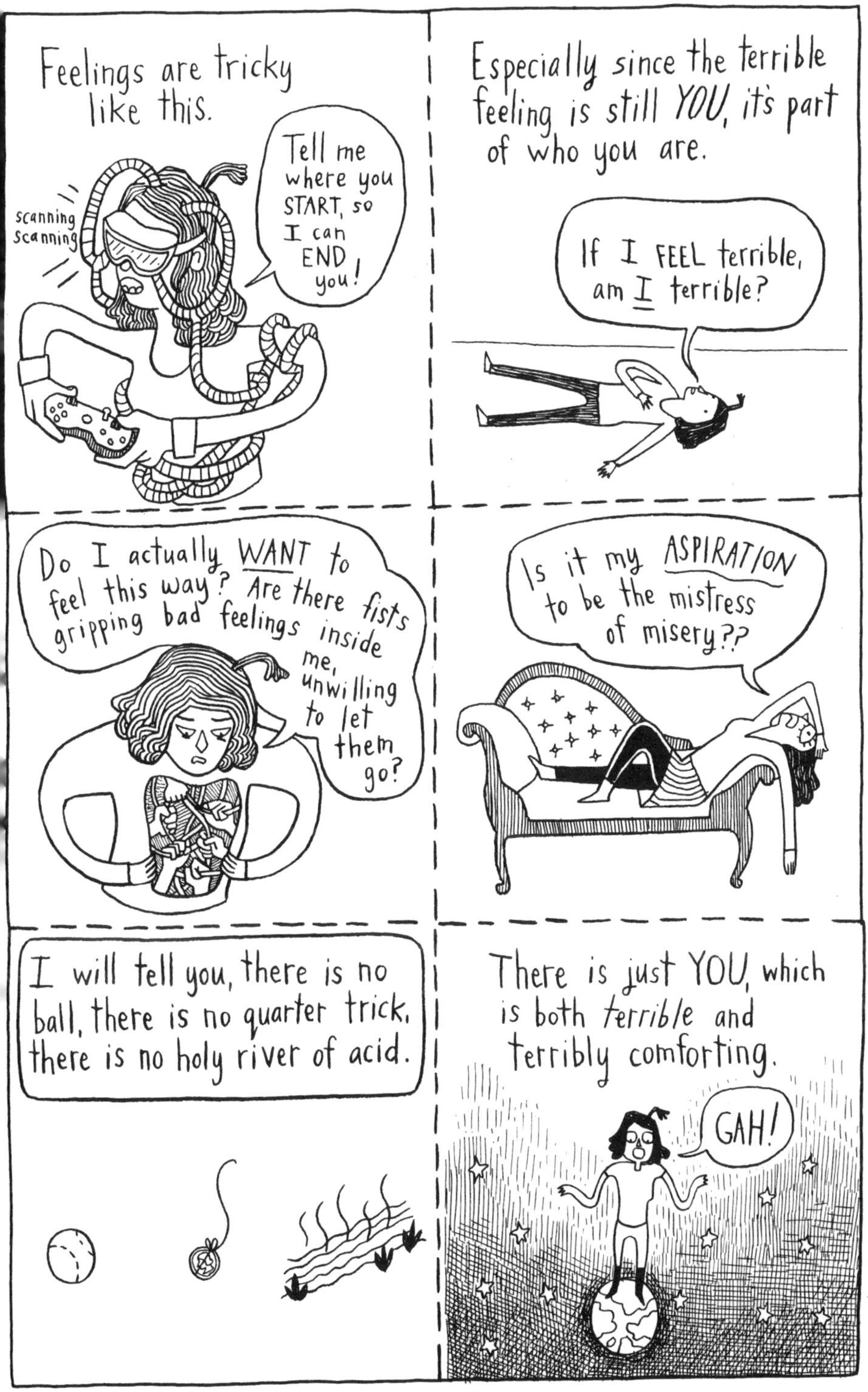

Feelings are tricky like this.
scanning scanning
Tell me where you START, so I can END you!
Especially since the terrible feeling is still YOU, it's part of who you are.
If I FEEL terrible, am I terrible?
Do I actually WANT to feel this way? Are there fists gripping bad feelings inside me, unwilling to let them go?
Is it my ASPIRATION to be the mistress of misery??
I will tell you, there is no ball, there is no quarter trick, there is no holy river of acid.
There is just YOU, which is both terrible and terribly comforting.
GAH!

And this is not a battle. Letting go is not a thing to be won, especially not through harshness.

It is not a thing to be expelled. It is not a thing that can be yanked or seized or grabbed.

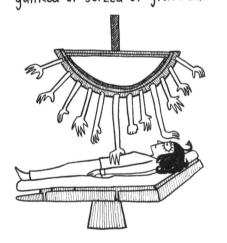

It is a slow thing that can be found by slowing down.

The awful feelings that haunt you can only be cornered with coaxes of well wishes.

Hello, heartache? Pushing you away isn't working.
Come over for tea.

It is an enemy you can only calm with care, with the kind of love one reserves for kittens and best friends and best friends of kittens.

Stay as long as you need to.

And that is the trick, REALLY, the con man's game. To tell yourself that EVERYTHING IS ALREADY OK, that you are ok with yourself, and EVERYTHING YOU THINK YOU SHOULD NOT FEEL.

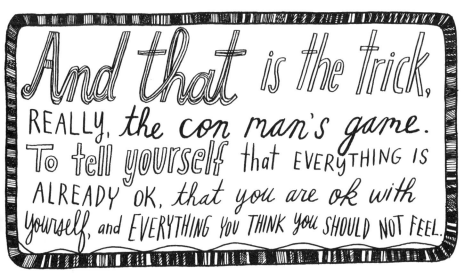

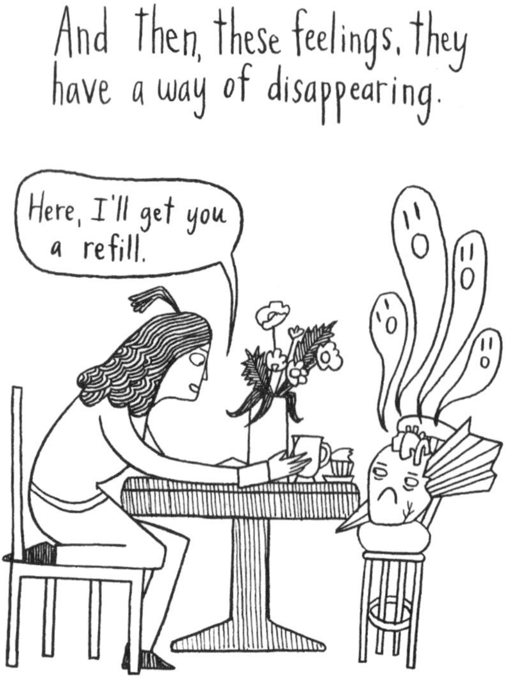
And then, these feelings, they have a way of disappearing.
Here, I'll get you a refill.

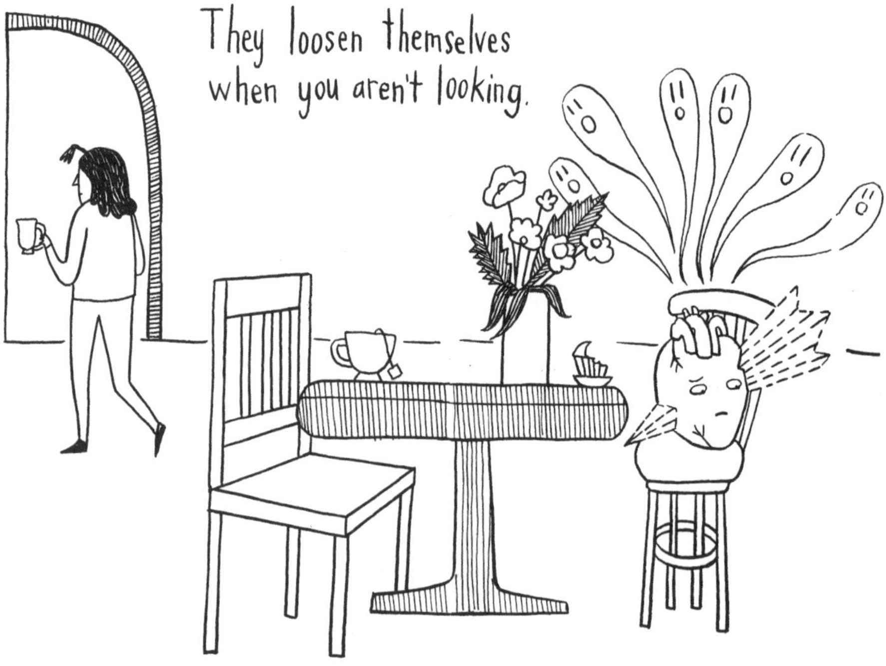
They loosen themselves when you aren't looking.

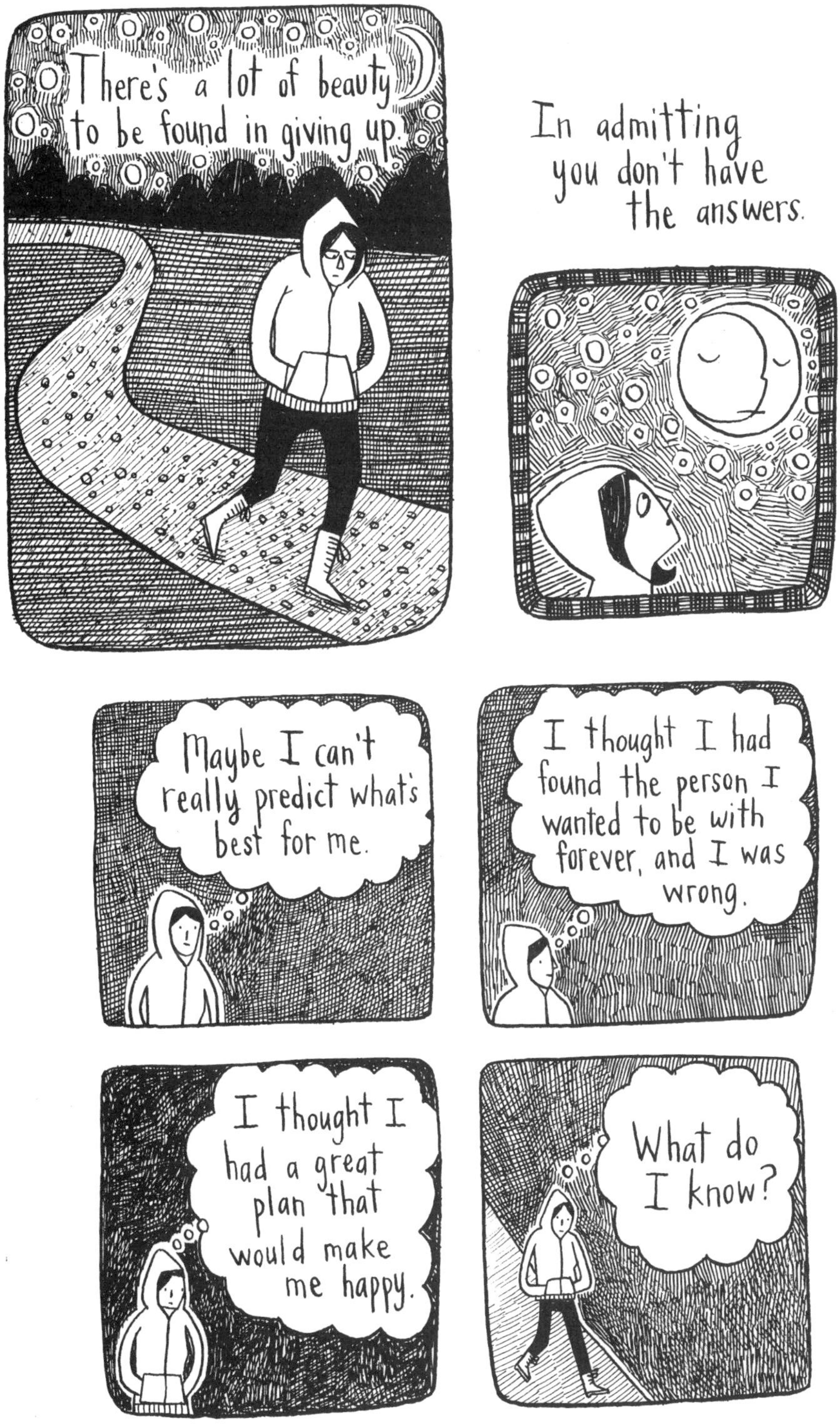
There's a lot of beauty to be found in giving up.
In admitting you don't have the answers.
Maybe I can't really predict what's best for me.
I thought I had found the person I wanted to be with forever, and I was wrong.
I thought I had a great plan that would make me happy.
What do I know?

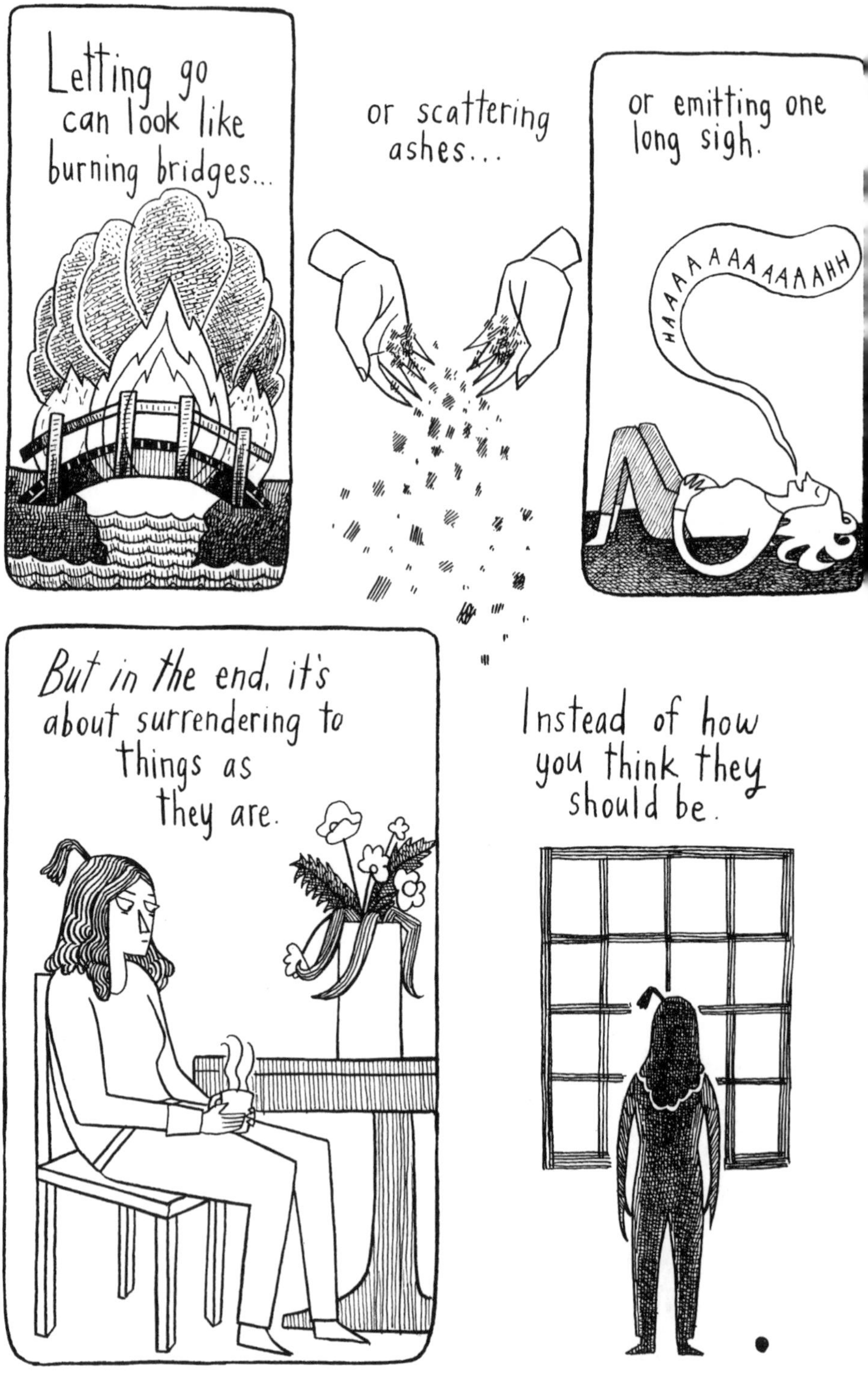
Letting go can look like burning bridges...
or scattering ashes...
or emitting one long sigh.
HAAAAAAAAAAAAAHH
But in the end, it's about surrendering to things as they are.
Instead of how you think they should be.

SAM READS AN EARLY DRAFT

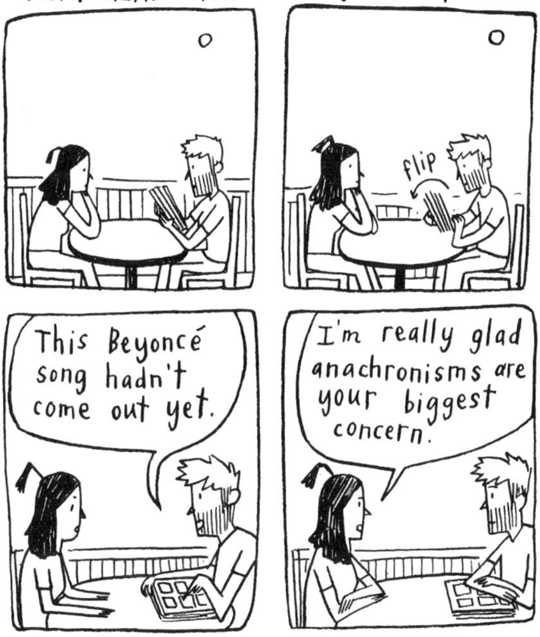
flip
This Beyoncé song hadn't come out yet.
I'm really glad anachronisms are your biggest concern.

Thank you, Sam, for loving me, and for your years of (sometimes complicated) friendship. Thank you for always encouraging my work, even when the resulting product might not paint you in the best light. And, ultimately, thank you for being the kind of person who was truly difficult to get over. My life is infinitely better for having had you in it.

-CORINNE